DATE DUE

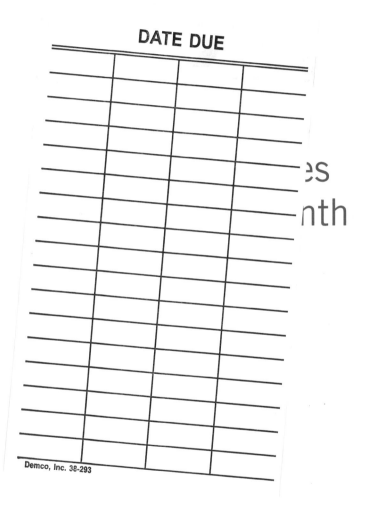

es

nth

Demco, Inc. 38-293

York Press

Tony Lythe is hereby identified as author of this work in accordance with Section 77 of the Copyright, Designs and Patents Act 1988

YORK PRESS
322 Old Brompton Road, London SW5 9JH

PEARSON EDUCATION LIMITED
Edinburgh Gate, Harlow,
Essex CM20 2JE, United Kingdom
Associated companies, branches and representatives throughout the world

First published 1999

ISBN 0–582–38195–9

Designed by Vicki Pacey
Phototypeset by Gem Graphics, Trenance, Mawgan Porth, Cornwall
Colour reproduction and film output by Spectrum Colour
Produced by Addison Wesley Longman China Limited, Hong Kong

CONTENTS

PREFACE

York Notes are designed to give you a broader perspective on works of literature studied at GCSE and equivalent levels. We have carried out extensive research into the needs of the modern literature student prior to publishing this new edition. Our research showed that no existing series fully met students' requirements. Rather than present a single authoritative approach, we have provided alternative viewpoints, empowering students to reach their own interpretations of the text. York Notes provide a close examination of the work and include biographical and historical background, summaries, glossaries, analyses of characters, themes, structure and language, cultural connections and literary terms.

If you look at the Contents page you will see the structure for the series. However, there's no need to read from the beginning to the end as you would with a novel, play, poem or short story. Use the Notes in the way that suits you. Our aim is to help you with your understanding of the work, not to dictate how you should learn.

York Notes are written by English teachers and examiners, with an expert knowledge of the subject. They show you how to succeed in coursework and examination assignments, guiding you through the text and offering practical advice. Questions and comments will extend, test and reinforce your knowledge. Attractive colour design and illustrations improve clarity and understanding, making these Notes easy to use and handy for quick reference.

York Notes are ideal for:
- Essay writing
- Exam preparation
- Class discussion

The author of this Note, Tony Lythe, has BA and MA degrees in English and American Literature, and is an examiner in English for A Level, GCSE and the International Baccalaureate. He has taught English for thirty years.

The text used in this Note is *The New Windmill Book of Mystery Stories of the Nineteenth Century* edited by Robert Etty (Heinemann, 1995).

Health Warning: **This study guide will enhance your understanding, but should not replace the reading of the original text and/or study in class.**

PART ONE

INTRODUCTION

HOW TO STUDY A SHORT STORY

You have bought this book because you want to study a collection of short stories, or an individual story, on your own. This may supplement work done in class.

- Try to read each story you are studying several times. The first reading should be fairly rapid to give you a basic understanding of the plot. Then read each story slowly and carefully more than once, making notes as you go along. Each reading will generate fresh ideas, and enable you to memorise details.
- Make thorough notes on the plot, themes, settings and characters in each story. Are there similarities between the stories? This is particularly important when you are studying several stories of the same type e. g. ghost stories or mystery stories. For instance, are the settings of ghost stories similar?
- How is each story told? Is it narrated by one of the people in the story, or by an all-seeing and all-knowing (**omniscient) narrator** (see Literary Terms), who is able to describe the emotions, behaviour and motivations of every character? What are the advantages and disadvantages of the chosen way of narrating a story?
- Which characters do you like or dislike? Why? Does the narrator tell you what to think about the characters or allow you to make up your own mind about them?
- A short story is different from a novel in lots of ways in addition to its length. What are the main differences? Consider why each author has chosen to write a short story rather than a novel. Would any of the stories benefit from being shorter or longer?

- Short stories need a strong beginning and end to contain the central idea or event. In a mystery story it is very important to have an effective climax, with perhaps a surprise or a **'twist in the tail'** (see Literary Terms). Which stories do this particularly well?
- Do you like or dislike any beginnings or endings of these stories?

To be effective, studying on your own requires self-discipline and careful planning. Good luck.

Although three of the authors of these short stories were not British (Ambrose Bierce and Edgar Allan Poe were American and Guy de Maupassant was French), the other writers lived most of their lives in Britain during the reign of Queen Victoria (1837–1901). It is important to understand the society in which these writers worked, not least because examiners look for an appreciation of the social, historical and cultural context of a text.

The Age of the Machine

By the time Victoria ascended the throne, the Industrial Revolution had already affected Britain profoundly. From being a predominantly rural, agricultural society, with the pace of life dictated by the speed of horses and humans, it became the 'Age of the Machine'. Hand looms in cottages gave way to factories, and horse-drawn transport was replaced by railways.

Agricultural workers flocked to the new towns which grew up around the factories. The consequent overcrowding led to serious health problems, crime and, often, an early death. In the 1840s, half of the children living in towns died before their fifth birthday.

The gap between rich and poor was immense. Half the land in Britain was owned by just 500 aristocrats, while many poor families struggled to exist on £25 a year. Servants figure strongly in these stories. The wage for a servant girl in the 1850s was about £8 a year. It was a class-dominated society, and one in which the poor were considered responsible for their poverty.

The penal system

One way the upper class attempted to retain its power was through the repressive penal system. Thomas Hardy's story, *The Three Strangers*, reminds us that people were hanged for sheep stealing in the 1820s. In fact, at that time, there were 200 crimes for which people could be executed, including picking pockets and stealing five shillings (25p) from a shop. However, by the 1840s, many of these had ceased to be capital crimes, with transportation to the colonies often used as an alternative.

Extension of suffrage

There were some changes in the political and social system in the nineteenth century. The right to vote was extended to most men by 1884 (although women had to wait until 1928), and the secret ballot was won in 1872. This extension of suffrage led to demands for the working class to be educated.

Growth of literacy

The landmark 1870 Education Act resulted in the establishment of schools for children up to the age of ten. Education was not free and universal until 1891, but the 1870 Act had considerable impact on literacy levels. Surveys suggest that in 1844 only 67% of men and 51% of women were able to write their names, but by 1891 these figures were 94% of men and 93% of women.

Not all of these could read fluently, but the second half of the nineteenth century saw a huge increase in the demand for reading material. To cater for this, the first public libraries appeared in the 1850s, and the abolition of taxes on newspapers further encouraged wider reading, as did the opening of W.H. Smith's bookshops on many railway stations.

Increased demand for short stories

There was a rapid growth in magazine publication. This created a demand for short stories, and many of the tales in this collection initially appeared in magazines such as *The Strand*, *All The Year Round* and *Household Words*, the last two edited by Charles Dickens, who provided an important outlet for ghost and mystery stories in the special Christmas editions of his magazines.

Many of these stories would originally have been read aloud to all the members of a household, which influenced the subject matter. The Victorian Age, at least superficially, was prudish about sexual matters, and conservative about the role of women in society. Authors writing about these subjects had to do so with tact and reticence.

The Victorian woman

For women, Victorian life was, by late-twentieth-century British standards, seriously restricted. The ideal of femininity, constructed mainly by men, was that women should be submissive and devote themselves to the welfare of home and family. The twentieth-century writer, Virginia Woolf, summarised the ideal of nineteenth-century womanhood as 'the Angel in the House who sacrificed herself daily to others'. The philosopher, John Stuart Mill, a supporter of women's equality, complained in *The Subjection of Women* (1869) that women were indoctrinated to believe 'submission', 'yielding to the control of others' and 'complete abnegation of themselves' were the ideal for women. Certainly women had little legal, political, social or economic power.

Reflecting the view of society, you will often find that the heroines of Victorian fiction exemplify patience and resignation to their fate, even when this involves suffering.

However, there was gradual and limited emancipation for some women. A few fee-paying girls' secondary schools opened, and there was greater opportunity for clerical and administrative work towards the end of the century.

Many women authors wrote ghost stories at this time because it enabled them to explore themes which they could not address in their other work, as Elizabeth Gaskell shows in *The Old Nurse's Story*.

Life remained physically hard for working-class women. It was only in 1842 that women and girls were legally prohibited from employment in the mines, and, until 1847, women could be employed for more than ten hours a day.

The Age of Doubt

The nineteenth century was a period of tremendous scientific and technological advance. In consequence, the Victorian Age was one of great anxiety and religious doubt, as many of the discoveries led people to question long-cherished beliefs. The crucial work, Charles Darwin's *On the Origin of Species* (1859), seemed to disprove scientifically that humans were a unique creation of God. If, as Darwin suggested, we have evolved from animals through chance and natural selection, much of the Bible became questionable. Other scientists queried the divinity of Jesus, and the concept of life after death.

Interest in the supernatural Paradoxically, this was also an era of widespread interest in spiritualism and the occult. Spirit mediums arrived from America, and seances were common. In 1882 The Society for Psychical Research was established, and Charles Dickens and Sir Arthur Conan Doyle, were active in the exploration of psychic phenomena. Several stories suggest there is an afterlife, from which ghosts return, in contradiction of the era's scepticism.

During the nineteenth century, mystery stories became very popular as offspring of the **Gothic novel** (see Literary Terms) and the **sensation novel** (see Literary Terms). To read about mysteries being solved had particular appeal for the Victorians, who craved security and certainty in a period when these were elusive.

PART TWO

SUMMARIES

DETAILED SUMMARIES

WILKIE COLLINS

Wilkie Collins, son of the painter, William Collins, was born in London in 1824. He trained as a barrister but started to write for magazines in the early 1850s after beginning a friendship with Charles Dickens. He wrote thirty novels, of which the most successful were *The Woman in White* (1860) and *The Moonstone* (1868), and is seen as the father of the British detective novel. He took opium to ease his gout, became an addict, and suffered ill-health for twenty years up to his death in 1889.

The Ostler

Note on page 1 the use of the present tense and the narrator's informal, conversational tone.

Arriving at an inn, the narrator is surprised to find the ostler asleep at midday. Obviously dreaming, the ostler shouts that he is being killed by a blonde woman. Later, the landlord tells the narrator the story of the ostler, Isaac Scatchard.

Isaac had been unlucky for most of his life. He had reached the age of forty without having a girlfriend, and still lived with his widowed mother.

Two days before his fortieth birthday, returning from an unsuccessful job interview, Isaac stays the night at a lonely inn. His sleep is disturbed by a dream of a grey-eyed, blonde-haired woman, who approaches his bed and, without speaking, tries to stab him. He wakes up screaming 'Murder' and the landlord, angry at being disturbed, turns him out.

At home next day, Isaac tells his mother his dream, and she is worried to learn the apparition appeared at 2 a.m., the time of her son's birth forty years earlier.

She notes the details of the 'dream woman' for future reference, as she knows Isaac will soon forget the incident.

A change in luck means Isaac enjoys seven years' successful employment before being granted a pension sufficient to provide comfortably for his mother and him.

Isaac seems dogged by bad luck. Can you think of all the times Fate seems to work against him?

One night, when they are celebrating his birthday, his mother asks Isaac to fetch her medicine from the chemist's. There he meets a woman leaving the shop, and the assistant tells him she has bought laudanum which he suspects she plans to use to kill herself.

Isaac speaks compassionately to her outside the shop, and she tells him his kindness has made her want to continue living. They arrange to meet the following day, and Isaac is soon passionately in love with the woman, Rebecca Murdoch.

Rebecca is the dominant partner, but, although he loves her intensely, Isaac never feels entirely at ease with her. Although Isaac is not very intelligent, he has an inkling he has seen Rebecca somewhere before.

As soon as Isaac's mother sees Rebecca, she recognises her as the woman in Isaac's dream, and begs him not to marry her, but he is not a man to break a promise.

Do you blame Isaac for marrying Rebecca in defiance of the dream, or respect his morality?

Initially their marriage is happy, but, as Isaac's birthday approaches, his wife changes. She becomes 'sullen' and 'contemptuous', and starts to drink heavily.

Isaac's dying mother visits the couple, hoping to mediate. She sees Rebecca cutting bread with an identical knife to the one in Isaac's dream. When Isaac asks Rebecca for the knife, she refuses, and he walks the streets all night, afraid to go home.

When Isaac's mother dies, Rebecca threatens to walk in the funeral procession. Isaac hits her and locks her in her room until the funeral is over. When he returns, Rebecca tells him that she is leaving him.

Isaac lies awake, fearing she will return to stab him. Seven nights later, just before 2 a.m. on his birthday, she does, but Isaac is ready, captures the knife, and flees. When he returns to the house she has gone, and Isaac suffers constant anxiety and nightmares, fearing another attack by Rebecca, especially each time his birthday approaches.

Comment

This complex story is capable of several interpretations. One view is that, through little fault of his own, the worthy Isaac is dogged by ill-luck and doomed to unhappiness, and the victim of a violent assault by a dominant, aggressive woman. In this interpretation Isaac contradicts stereotypes of masculinity.

Remember the landlord, and therefore we the readers, have heard only Isaac's version of events.

However, it is very important to see things from Rebecca's perspective. She has to confront an overprotective mother-son relationship. As we presume she did not know of the dream, Rebecca must have felt profound rejection at Mrs Scatchard's behaviour on their first meeting.

Later she faces physical abuse from her husband, and the stigma against women who misuse alcohol. It is not in any way to condone her violent response to suggest Rebecca suffered too.

Wilkie Collins wrote an article about the representation of blonde women in Victorian literature. He challenges the stereotype here.

Although we condemn Rebecca's violence, we may be attracted by the fact that she is more assertive than most Victorian women, which is why she is seen as a threat. We applaud her refusal to tolerate physical violence from her husband in a society where male abuse in marriage was often tacitly accepted. She was described as the dominant partner in the relationship, confirming her status as a figure of fear for male readers.

Perhaps Isaac's dream dramatises the fears of many Victorian men about the emasculation they would suffer at the hands of assertive 'new women'. Also, as a 'lady', she would be a fantasy figure for the working-class Isaac.

Do Isaac's good qualities, such as his devotion and refusal to break promises, cause his unhappiness?

The relationship between Isaac and his mother is very supportive and she is one of the many Victorian women who devoted their lives to a man's welfare. However, she may represent the dangers of overprotective motherhood, for there are times when she still treats him like a child. Perhaps, as Wilkie Collins emphasises Isaac's intellectual limitations, she feels she has to protect him, but she may be to blame for his naïve behaviour.

There is a strong sense that events are predetermined and that Isaac's is a premonitory dream. It saved his life in warning him of an attack and showing the knife's hiding place. In sharp contrast to his mother, he ignores the supernatural and pays a price, but, if events are predetermined, how could he have altered his destiny?

GLOSSARY   **ostler** person responsible for stabling horses at an inn

tap-room room where alcohol is sold and drunk

tallow hard animal fat used in candles

preternatural exceptional

clasp-knife folding knife

buck-horn horn of male deer

rush-candle candle made from dipping a rush in tallow

your score on the slate Isaac's bill was chalked on a slate

laudanum alcoholic tincture of opium

pick-lock skeleton key or sharp object

heard of yet heard of since

Elizabeth Gaskell

Elizabeth Gaskell (née Stevenson) was born in London in 1810, but her mother died a year later, and she was raised by an aunt in Knutsford, Cheshire. In 1832 she married William Gaskell, a Unitarian minister, and helped him with his pastoral work in deprived areas of Manchester. She turned to writing only after the death of her infant son, but her first novel, *Mary Barton* (1848), brought her to Charles Dickens's attention. Elizabeth Gaskell subsequently published several novels and short stories, the latter occasionally showing her interest in the supernatural. She died in 1865.

The Old Nurse's Story

Note the detailed description of the grounds and house, giving the ghost story a solid, realistic setting.

Hester, an old family nurse, tells Rosamond's children about their mother when she was a child. Hester was first employed as a girl to nurse Rosamond, whose parents died when she was about five. Rosamond's mother was Lord Furnivall's granddaughter, so, when she was orphaned, Rosamond and Hester went to live in a large manor house belonging to the Furnivall family. Apart from the servants, the only inhabitants are the aged Grace Furnivall, and her companion, Mrs Stark.

Hester and Rosamond enjoy exploring the old house, apart from the perpetually-locked east wing. One day, accompanied by Dorothy, the friendly housekeeper, they see the portrait of the beautiful and haughty young Grace Furnivall. Dorothy shows Hester the portrait of Maude, Grace's even more beautiful sister, which has mysteriously been turned to face the wall.

As winter comes, Hester hears music from the huge organ in the hall. Bessy, the maid, tells Hester the long-dead Lord Furnivall is playing. Hester is convinced the noise is supernatural when she discovers the organ is broken. As the weather worsens, the organ music grows louder and wilder.

Dorothy and the kitchen are havens of warmth and light; Mrs Furnivall and Mrs Stark are sad, cold and hopeless. What is the significance of Miss Furnivall's deafness?

Rosamond becomes a favourite of the two old ladies, but goes missing one snowy afternoon when Hester is in church. After searching the house desperately, outside in the moonlight Hester sees tiny footprints in the snow leading up the Fells. As Hester races up in pursuit, she is met by a shepherd carrying an unconscious Rosamond, whom he had found asleep under a holly tree.

Next day, fully recovered, Rosamond tells Hester that, the previous afternoon, a pretty girl had beckoned her to follow up the hill, where they found a lady weeping under a holly tree, who had taken Rosamond in her arms and rocked her to sleep. Everyone is shocked by this story and Mrs Stark warns, 'Keep her [Rosamond] from that child. It will lure her to her death'.

A few weeks later Rosamond claims to see the same little girl outside the house in the snow, and this time Hester also sees her. As she rushes to the door, the noise of the organ swells. Hester hustles Rosamond to the kitchen, to the terrified servants, where Dorothy tells Hester the phantom child's origins.

Many years previously, Grace and Maude had fallen in love with a foreign musician employed by their father. The musician married Maude secretly, and, unknown to anyone, she gave birth to his daughter at a farm on the moor. The musician continued to flirt with Grace, causing increasing jealousy between the sisters, until he tired of this and departed, never to return.

The sisters lived separate lives, Maude in the east wing and Grace in the west wing. Their father became increasingly infirm and had to use a crutch. Eventually, Maude boasted to her sister about her marriage, and an anguished Grace vowed vengeance.

Maude made weekly visits to her daughter on the farm, before secretly bringing the child to live with her in the east wing. Grace told her father about Maude's marriage, and, after a terrible row, during which he hit his grandchild with his crutch, he turned them out on a freezing night, warning the servants not to assist them. Grace stood beside him, looking smug.

The next morning, shepherds found a crazy Maude nursing her dead child, victim of the cold. The old lord never played the organ again and died within a year.

The narrative technique is interesting. Hester tells the reader what Dorothy has told her, so it is a second-hand account.

When Dorothy has finished this story, a terrified Hester realises the phantom child is the ghost of Maude's daughter and covers all the windows to stop Rosamond seeing her outside.

One night, the house is disturbed by screams and shouts from the east wing. Hester has to restrain Rosamond from rushing there. Suddenly the ghost of Lord Furnivall appears, driving out the ghosts of Maude and her child. Rosamond tries to go to the phantom child, but faints when Lord Furnivall hits his grandchild with his crutch. The figure of the young Grace appears, looking triumphant. The old Grace, seeing all this, collapses and dies, muttering, 'What is done in youth can never be undone in age!'

COMMENT   This magnificent story of the supernatural is unusual in being narrated by a woman servant. The Victorian view

How does Mrs Gaskell convince us that Hester is a reliable narrator?

was that women were emotional, and therefore unreliable narrators of ghost stories, which should be recounted by respectable, professional men, whose opinions could be trusted.

The story is about the consequences of evil acts. Grace is jealous of her sister, seeks revenge by revealing her marriage and child, and consequently an innocent child dies. The phantom child seeks to lure the latest member of the disgraced Furnivall family to her death, so perpetuating the cycle of revenge, but she is saved by the selfless love of Hester, who is untainted by the evil of the aristocratic family. In the stunning **dénouement** (see Literary Terms) Grace is forced to face up to the consequence of her actions. Her final words are the moral message of the story.

As narrator, Hester gives a female, working-class perspective on aristocratic life. Her real importance though is in demonstrating that her love for Rosamond can defeat evil forces. It is unusual to find a heroine in danger (Rosamond) being rescued, not by a powerful man, but by the strength of a woman's love.

The story reveals the destructive emotions behind the facade of the Victorian country house, showing that outwardly-respectable families had hidden secrets. Behind locked doors, aristocratic families hid the consequences of sexual passion and relationships with 'unsuitable' members of a 'lower' class.

The grand organ, which is broken inside, is probably intended to be a symbol

The main focus for criticism is Lord Furnivall, the Victorian patriarch. He treats his daughters cruelly and dictatorially. His heartless exercise of power and control (based entirely on his male gender) shows that self-determination was denied even to upper-class women.

Note the vivid descriptions of the old women and the marvellous **simile** (see Literary Terms) of the wrinkles on Grace Furnivall's face 'as if they had been drawn all over it with a needle's point' (p. 29).

Being a skilled craftswoman, Elizabeth Gaskell does not make the daughters innocent victims of a cruel father, for they are as vindictive, proud and haughty as he. However, Maude and her daughter are the victims of a male-dominated society. Both sisters suffer because of the fickleness of the husband and lover who deserts them. Indeed, a **feminist critique** (see Literary Terms) of the story would suggest that the sisters' problems arise because they compete for a man rather than seek fulfilment in their sisterly relationship.

GLOSSARY   **massy andirons** large firedogs

trumpet trumpet-shaped tube used as a hearing aid

stomacher the jewelled or embroidered pointed front of a woman's dress

'Flesh is grass' Isaiah 40:6 in the Bible reads 'All flesh is grass'

gowk (dialect) a fool

soughing the softly moaning sound of the wind

bairn child

warming-pan flat, closed, long-handled brass vessel holding hot coals for warming a bed

I shall catch it I shall be in trouble

lord's ward under the legal guardianship of Lord Furnivall

Sir Arthur Conan Doyle

Arthur Conan Doyle was born in Edinburgh in 1859. He practised as a doctor for several years before writing his first Sherlock Holmes novel, *A Study in Scarlet*, in 1887. He subsequently wrote many stories about the detective, who made him rich and famous. Arthur Conan Doyle was knighted in 1902. He was interested in spiritualism in later life. He died in 1930.

The
Adventure of
the Engineer's
Thumb

Victor Hatherley, an hydraulics engineer, arrives at Dr Watson's home early one morning, with a handkerchief wrapped around his hand to protect his severed thumb. He tells Watson some people had tried to murder him the previous night. The doctor believes it is a case for his good friend, the eminent detective, Sherlock Holmes.

Note the
journalistic style of
reporting events
in a detached
fashion.

In Holmes's house, Hatherley tells them he is a bachelor and orphan, who started his own business a couple of years previously. He had had little work, so was delighted when, the previous evening, Colonel Lysander Stark had offered him the large sum of 50 guineas to visit his house late that night to inspect a malfunctioning hydraulic press which, he claimed, was used to extract fuller's earth. He pledged Hatherley to absolute secrecy, which made the engineer suspicious, but the large fee was too attractive for him to refuse the work.

Stark meets Hatherley at a country station and they drive to a large house which they reach after midnight. When Stark leaves Hatherley alone, a foreign woman, Elise, urges him to leave 'before it is too late!'.

He ignores her and is taken to the faulty machine by Stark and his manager, Mr Ferguson. Hatherley quickly diagnoses the fault. He is inspecting a suspicious substance on the machine's floor when Stark sees him and attempts to crush him in the machine, but Hatherley escapes through the side walls. Elise leads him to an upstairs balcony, from which he can jump into the garden and escape.

As Hatherley is dangling from the balcony by his fingertips, Stark attacks him with a machete, severing his thumb, and he falls into the bushes below.

When he regains consciousness, he is surprised to find himself by the road near the station, where Elise and Ferguson had dragged him. He catches a train to Paddington, and goes to Dr Watson's house.

Using his deductive skills, Holmes manages to locate Stark's house, but, when he arrives, it is on fire. The criminals have disappeared, but the police are certain they have used the hydraulic press to counterfeit coins.

COMMENT   Sherlock Holmes does not appear prominently in this story, but his deductive reasoning, as usual, solves the case. He is not at his most sparkling, and it is not a strong plot. The ending comes as an anti-climax; the dramatic escape of Hatherley is the real climax.

What do you think of Hatherley's behaviour?   The severed thumb is the sort of gruesome detail popular in **sensation novels** (see Literary Terms). It is Hatherley's punishment for colluding in Stark's plan to trick his neighbours, and for his greediness in accepting disreputable work because of high financial rewards. He ignores Elise's warning but redeems himself somewhat by his later act of chivalry to her.

Is Elise's lamp a symbol of anything?   It is Elise who urges the men to behave better and act with greater compassion. In this respect she conforms with the stereotype of Victorian womanhood. The criminals would have been detested by the materialistic Victorians because counterfeiting devalued real money.

Sir Arthur Conan Doyle conveys his distaste by stressing Stark's abnormal thinness and exploits the xenophobia of the English middle class by making his criminal German.

GLOSSARY

en bloc all at the same time

civil practice Watson had been in the armed forces

Bohemian informal and unconventional

dooties duties

carbolized impregnated with carbolic acid, an antiseptic

hansom a two-wheeled, horse-drawn cab for two passengers

dottles remnants of unburnt tobacco

hydraulic stamping machine a machine in which a force is applied to a fluid to create a greater pressure

fuller's earth type of clay used in fulling (cleaning and thickening) freshly-woven cloth

commonplace book book into which memorable extracts from other books are copied

9th inst. ninth day of the current month

boxed the compass mentioned all points of the compass

coiners makers of counterfeit coins

Identify the speaker.

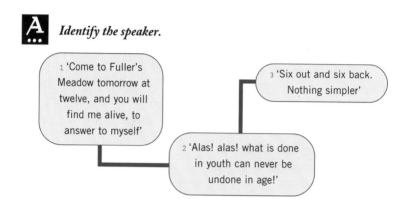

1 'Come to Fuller's Meadow tomorrow at twelve, and you will find me alive, to answer to myself'

3 'Six out and six back. Nothing simpler'

2 'Alas! alas! what is done in youth can never be undone in age!'

Identify the person(s) 'to whom' these comments refer.

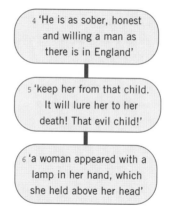

4 'He is as sober, honest and willing a man as there is in England'

5 'keep her from that child. It will lure her to her death! That evil child!'

6 'a woman appeared with a lamp in her hand, which she held above her head'

Check your answers on page 93.

B *Consider these issues.*

a The role of the supernatural in *The Ostler*. Does the dream save Isaac's life or condemn him to a life of misery?

b Family and gender relationships in *The Ostler* and *The Old Nurse's Story*.

c The advantages and drawbacks of having more than one narrator in a story.

EDGAR ALLAN POE

Edgar Allan Poe's parents were both actors when he was born in Boston, USA, in 1809, but he was orphaned two years later. He lived in London from 1815 to 1820, then spent the rest of his life in North America, editing newspapers and writing poems and short stories. In the early 1840s he wrote some of the first detective stories, including *The Murders in the Rue Morgue* (1841), and several early horror stories. Edgar Allan Poe lived a tempestuous life of drink, love affairs and bitter quarrels, before his death in 1849.

The Pit and the Pendulum

The narrator, charged with heresy by the Inquisition, faints when sentenced to death. When he regains consciousness, he is in a damp, clammy, pitch-black dungeon. As he explores his prison, he falls at the edge of a deep well, which saves him from the intended death. He is afraid there are other pits nearby, but manages to grope his way to the wall without further mishap.

What are the purposes and effects of Poe's extensive use of question marks, exclamation marks and dashes in this story?

He awakes to find himself strapped to a wooden frame, able to move only his head and arm. Having added strong spices to his food, his captors have withdrawn his water, so he is desperately thirsty.

After a while, he looks up, and is horrified to see a large pendulum, with a razor-sharp base, hanging directly over him. Soon after, he notices the pendulum has descended, and realises, to avoid certain death, he will have to escape quickly.

He has a brainwave. His prison is overrun by hungry rats, so, if he smears some of his meat on the ropes which hold him, he reasons the rats will eat it and gnaw through the ropes. Just as the pendulum starts to cut into his body, the rats gnaw through the last rope, and he is able to roll out of the way. The pendulum is immediately retracted, proving he is being observed.

Having escaped this, he is faced by a new threat. The walls of his prison start to glow, and there is a smell of hot iron. He rushes towards the pit to escape the heat. He is terrified to see that the cell is changing shape, with the walls moving in on him, forcing him towards the pit. As he is teetering on the edge of the pit, he utters a final scream and, at that moment, his arm is grabbed by his rescuers, the French army.

COMMENT   As it documents the cruelty and ingenuity of dictatorial regimes in torturing those who do not accept the 'party line', this story is relevant for our time, which has seen governments using similar tactics to control dissidents.

How does Edgar Allan Poe convey the narrator's hysterical mental state?   Sensory deprivation, when a person cannot see or hear anything, is itself an instrument of torture, and that he is constantly being watched compounds his agony. To this is added the anguish of knowing that a quick death is unlikely, a lingering one certain, and escape impossible. It is no wonder the narrator is on the verge of insanity.

The terrors of the Inquisition had the fascination for the nineteenth century that the activities of notorious serial killers have for the twentieth. Edgar Allan Poe read books on the tortures and, in this story, he uses several literary accounts (of the pit, the pendulum and the moving walls). Although it is a genuinely horrific tale, it is largely derivative.

The use of the past tense means some loss of impact, and the narrator admits he can only vaguely recall the events. You may also find Edgar Allan Poe's style over-elaborate and artificial, especially in the first part of the story. Examining the first fifteen lines on page 72 will illustrate this. He uses **rhetorical questions** (see Literary Terms) freely, and long **subordinate clauses** (see Literary Terms) separated by semicolons, extend the main idea, which is sometimes lost in the process.

The vocabulary is traditional and even **archaic** (see Literary Terms).

Edgar Allan Poe adopted his style from contemporary magazines – a **first person narrator** (see Literary Terms) describing horrific experiences. However, this narrator is preoccupied with his mental state, although, in fairness, as his torture involves sensory deprivation, all he can describe is the working of his body and mind.

Note the use of onomatopoeia in 'hissed' (p. 79), and the use of 'Down' three times for emphasis on page 81.

Edgar Allan Poe compensates for the absence of visual descriptions by some **evocative** (see Literary Terms) vocabulary to communicate the feel of the cell: e.g. 'smooth', 'slimy' and 'cold' (p. 74); 'moist' and 'slippery' (p. 75); and 'close' and 'clammy' (p. 76).

The story is successful because it exploits some of our deepest fears and nightmares, in the manner of many later horror stories. Edgar Allan Poe knew this and merely triggers our imagination.

Occasionally he gives us gruesome detail: e.g. The rats 'writhed upon my throat; their cold lips sought my own' (p. 83). We shudder at the thought, and the verb 'writhe' is very powerful.

The ending is **melodramatic** (see Literary Terms) and improbable, but, given the narrator's sense of hopelessness, it provides a genuinely unexpected '**twist in the tail**' (see Literary Terms).

GLOSSARY

Impia tortorum etc this is all invention by Edgar Allan Poe

that long agony his trial for heresy by the court of the Inquisition

sable sable fur was originally brown but would have been dyed black. It was much sought-after and expensive

seven tall candles this recalls the seven (a mystic number) candlesticks in the Apocalypse

galvanic battery a primary battery for producing an electrical current

Hades in Greek mythology Hades was the underworld where
spirits went after death

Toledo city on the river Tagus and a centre of the Inquisition

most hideous of fates Edgar Allan Poe was terrified of being
buried alive. He wrote a story called *The Premature Burial*

monkish ingenuity inventiveness of the monks of the Inquisition

recusant someone who refuses to submit to authority or comply
with a regulation

my deliverers i.e. the rats

General Lassalle Lassalle was the general of the French army
which captured Toledo during the Peninsular War in 1808

MARY E. BRADDON

Mary E. Braddon was born in London in 1837. Her
parents separated when she was three. She was an
actress for three years before publishing *Lady Audley's
Secret* (1862), which made her name, and the author of
more than seventy novels, many of which were best-
sellers. Mary E. Braddon had six children and five
stepchildren, and died in 1915.

*Samuel
Lowgood's
Revenge*

The story begins in the reign of George the Second
when Samuel Lowgood, the narrator, and Christopher
Weldon are junior clerks in a firm of ship owners.
Samuel, a poor, insignificant orphan, is jealous of the
rich, foppish, handsome Christopher.

*Note the contrast
between the dark
surroundings and
Christopher's fair
skin and hair.*

Owing to his family connections, and despite being lazy
and incompetent, Christopher has reached, after four
weeks, the same status in the office as Samuel has after
ten years' hard work. Samuel is most envious of
Christopher's blossoming relationship with Lucy
Malden, who lives opposite the office. Samuel has loved
Lucy for years, and hopes to marry her when he's
promoted at work. Christopher courts Lucy, singing
and playing his flute for her, while Samuel constantly
thinks of revenge.

One day, after mocking Samuel for his shabby clothes,
Christopher shows him a tailor's bill for a large sum.
If it is not paid within two weeks, Christopher's mother
will be informed. Samuel spies on Christopher and
sees him practising the signature used on the firm's
cheques.

A couple of days later, Samuel surreptitiously observes
Christopher leaving the firm's bank. Making enquiries
there, Samuel discovers Christopher has withdrawn £40
from the firm's account by forging the official signature.
Samuel uses his life savings to repay the £40 to the
bank in return for the cheque, with which he plans to
discredit Christopher at a later date. He hides the
cheque in a locked chest. Christopher is soon promoted
to the London office on double the salary, leaving a
heart-broken Lucy behind.

Ten years later, when he has become chief clerk in the
office, Lucy unenthusiastically accepts Samuel's offer of
marriage, while Christopher marries a nobleman's
daughter and becomes a partner in the firm.
Christopher and his wife plan to take over the
Lowgoods' house after extensive refurbishment.

A grand dinner party is arranged to celebrate
Christopher's promotion, attended by the firm's senior

staff, at which Samuel plans to hand the forged cheque to the head of the firm, disgracing Christopher in his moment of triumph.

On the eve of the party, Samuel dreams the cheque has been lost. He is relieved to find the chest's key in its usual place around his neck. However, when he searches for the cheque before leaving for the dinner, it has gone. He is so upset that he is confined to bed for nine weeks with brain fever.

Is Lucy (her name suggests light) the good woman who saves Samuel from his immoral pursuit of revenge?

Some years later, Lucy dies. On her death bed she tells Samuel that she had once saved him from committing a great wrong. She had heard him sleep-talking about his planned revenge, and the location of the cheque, which she subsequently removed. Lucy gives Samuel the forged cheque, which he passes to Christopher at her funeral.

COMMENT

This is only marginally a mystery story because, although we have a premonitory dream, it does not have great significance in the plot.

An elderly narrator looks back on the experiences of youth. Now that he is not in the throes of his passion for revenge, Samuel can be quite detached, and manages a degree of self-criticism and self-awareness. However, as Samuel narrates the story, albeit from the perspective of old age, everything is seen through his eyes.

Samuel spies on Christopher, tells lies, delights in telling Lucy that Christopher has left her, and vindictively delays exposing Christopher's crime.

Mary E. Braddon has not simplified the characters into good and bad. Although we have a lot of sympathy for Samuel, and his envy of someone who has everything so easily strikes a chord with many of us, he is not a very attractive character.

The story's moral and social messages are disturbing. It seems that crime pays, and connections and style are more important than ability and hard work. Linked

Are the names
Lowgood and
Weldon
significant?

with this is a strong criticism of the class system in Victorian Britain. Christopher rises by nepotism while Samuel faces barriers whatever he does. It casts doubt on the Victorians' belief in the importance of initiative and self-help.

The institution of marriage is also scrutinised. The Victorians would have been shocked that Lucy acts out of romantic love for Christopher rather than out of duty to her husband, though the blow may have been softened because she claims to be saving her husband from a sinful act.

GLOSSARY

King George the Second King of Great Britain 1727–60

maccaroni fashionable young man (originally reserved for men who had visited Italy)

court-sword ceremonial sword worn over formal dress

doubly an orphan both his parents had died. In contrast, Christopher is 'an orphan' because only his father had died

corn chandler a dealer in corn

sacques loose, full-length gown, coat, or pleated silk appendage attached to the shoulders of a dress

pannier-hoops hoops in a skirt around the hips

Mr Henry Fielding eighteenth-century novelist who wrote *Tom Jones* (1749), which describes the bawdy adventures of an attractive young man

sconces wall brackets to hold candlesticks

William and Mary William of Orange and his wife, Mary, ruled Great Britain from 1688 to 1694

dimity cotton cloth, woven with raised patterns.

stuff woollen cloth

new opera about thieves John Gay (1685–1732) wrote two operas, *The Beggar's Opera* (1728) and *Polly* (1729), both referred to in the story

scraped acquaintance insinuated himself into the father's friendship

Cease your funning eighteenth-century song
spade guineas gold coins to the value of 21 shillings (£1.05p)
  minted between 1787 and 1799 with a spade stamped on the
  back
lawn cravat a cravat (neck-scarf) made from fine linen called
  lawn
sedan chair a covered seat, carried by two bearers, back and
  front

CHARLES DICKENS

Charles Dickens was born in Portsmouth in 1812.
His nurse told him terrifying stories of the macabre
and supernatural, and he was an avid reader of the
'penny-dreadful' comics. He had a secure childhood
until his father was imprisoned for debt, and young
Charles had to work in a miserable blacking warehouse
in London. Later, he became a Parliamentary reporter,
and eventually was able to devote himself to writing
fiction, editing magazines and giving readings of his
work. Of his many novels, *David Copperfield*
(1849–50), *Great Expectations* (1860–1) and *Oliver
Twist* (1837–9) are the most accessible. Charles
Dickens was fascinated by the supernatural (using it
most famously in *A Christmas Carol* – 1843), interested
in mesmerism (hypnotism) and attended at least one
seance. He died in 1870.

*The
Signalman*

The narrator (we know from other stories he is
nicknamed Barbox Brothers, the company for which he
used to work) is strolling one evening when he notices a
signal box in a deep cutting near a tunnel. The 'dark,
sallow' signalman is standing in the doorway holding a
flag, and Barbox greets him, 'Halloa! Below there!'. He
is surprised the strange-looking signalman responds by
looking down the line rather than upwards towards
him.

The signalman initially thinks Barbox is the ghost, which explains his odd behaviour.

When Barbox climbs down to the signal box, he notices what a 'solitary and dismal place' it is, and is puzzled why the signalman is standing rapt on the line. During the ensuing conversation, Barbox finds it so difficult to engage the signalman in conversation that he wonders if he is a ghost or mentally ill. Ironically, the signalman is wary of Barbox because he thinks his visitor is the ghost who has been haunting him!

When he is reassured Barbox is human, the signalman tells him he had studied physics in his youth, but had run wild and had not made the most of his opportunities. Barbox notices what a conscientious and vigilant worker he is, but is puzzled because he twice reacts to the alarm bell when it hasn't rung. The signalman admits he is very troubled about something, but will not elaborate. Promising to return the following evening, Barbox leaves, perplexed about why the signalman begs him not to speak as he leaves the cutting.

The following evening, the signalman describes his problem. One moonlit night, about a year earlier, he had seen a figure standing near the tunnel waving and shouting, 'Halloa! Below there!' and 'Look out!'. When the signalman had rushed to the tunnel to investigate the danger, the figure had disappeared. Telegraph messages in both directions had indicated there was no danger on the line, but, within a few hours, there was a fatal train crash in the tunnel.

Some months later, the ghostly figure had returned, this time covering his face in a gesture of mourning. That day, a young woman had died as the train passed the signal box.

The signalman is desperately anxious because the ghost has recently reappeared, shouting warnings and ringing the warning bell. The phantom had appeared during the narrator's visit on the previous day, but Barbox hadn't seen 'him' or heard the bell.

Do you think it is significant that the signalman was once a science student?

The signalman is at the end of his tether. His employers would think him mad if he issued a warning but couldn't identify the danger. However, as the phantom had proved prophetic the previous times, he takes the warning seriously. Barbox manages to calm him, and offers to stay the night, but the signalman declines, so the narrator leaves at 2 a.m., promising to return the following night.

Barbox is worried about his own responsibilities, for the signalman's state of mind means he may not be able to do his job properly. He decides to offer to accompany him to the doctor's.

When he returns to the cutting the following evening, he is horrified to see a figure with his left sleeve across his eyes, waving his right arm, but relieved the figure is a man and not a spirit. There are other men nearby, and a tarpaulin over the track. When he climbs down, he learns the signalman had been killed by an engine that morning. The driver had shouted the warning, 'Below there! Look out ! Look out! For God's sake clear the way,' which were exactly the phantom's words, and had put one hand over his eyes and waved the other. The narrator is stunned that the engine driver had not only used exactly the phantom's words, but also the identical words he (Barbox) had uttered to himself when the signalman described the ghost (p. 111).

COMMENT   *The Signalman* first appeared in the 1866 Christmas edition of Charles Dickens's magazine, *All the Year Round*, with other railway stories, under the collective title *Mugby Junction*. Most were narrated by the recently-retired Barbox Brothers.

1250 men hacked out the one-and-a-half-mile Kilsby tunnel, lit by only torches and candles. Twenty-seven died.

Whereas most nineteenth-century ghost stories had traditional settings in graveyards or old haunted houses, this has a modern, and, for the time, 'high tech' setting. Railways and tunnels were still novel and exciting in the 1860s, but Charles Dickens saw trains as dangerous and destructive. In his novel *Dombey and Son* (1846–8), Carker is killed by a train.

The setting for *The Signalman* is probably Clayton Tunnel under the South Downs where a fatal accident occurred in 1861. Charles Dickens was a passenger in a train crash at Staplehurst in 1865, in which many people died.

On page 106 Charles Dickens describes the train's 'violent pulsation' and onomatopoeic 'rush'. What is the effect?

A central issue in the story is that, as the ghost is warning of a future event, does it mean it will inevitably happen? If so, what is the point of the ghost's appearances? The Victorians liked their ghosts to have some purpose, (usually to punish past misdeeds) but spirits who warn about the future have no obvious function if the event is predetermined and inevitable. As the signalman asks, why has the ghost come? 'Why not go to somebody with credit to be believed and power to act?' (p. 116).

An important discussion is whether human events are chance happenings or predetermined. Initially it appears chance that Barbox is strolling near the tunnel, and that, in shielding his eyes from the sun, he adopts an identical pose to the ghost's, and repeats 'his' exact words. This 'chance' makes the signalman suspect Barbox is the ghost, act strangely, and stimulate the narrator's interest in his situation. However, the story's final sentence suggests these may not be chance events, but a predetermined supernatural process, of which Barbox is a part.

In describing the cutting, Charles Dickens draws parallels with Hell and Hades. He writes, 'The cutting was extremely deep, and unusually precipitous' (p. 106). He makes us feel it and smell it. 'Clammy' stone becomes 'oozier and wetter' as the narrator scrambles down, and this becomes a 'dripping-wet wall of jagged stone,' with 'an earthy, deadly smell' (p. 106). This accumulation of details makes the cutting seem unpleasant and tomb-like.

Dickens's technique in this story is often to write obliquely and suggestively without being explicit: e.g. 'There was something remarkable ... said for my life what' (p. 105).

Charles Dickens cleverly sustains suspense. Note how the signalman at the first meeting will not reveal what is troubling him. As in serials and 'soap operas', revelations are delayed until the following night. Charles Dickens maintains suspense by suggesting something exciting is to come. The signalman says, 'I am troubled, sir ... It is very very difficult to speak of' (p.109). Charles Dickens knows the power of suggestion and merely hints that the story will be strange and dramatic.

Tension is intensified by the signalman's bizarre request that Barbox should not say anything when he leaves. Both Barbox and the reader wonder why this is so important to the signalman.

By detaching himself from the world, the signalman is allowing himself to be prey to gloom and the supernatural, and divorced from the redeeming power of human love. It is **ironic** (see Literary Terms) that the signalman dies because he is so conscientious, and is so worried about how to respond to the ghost that he becomes careless about himself.

The narrator learns that inaction can be as destructive as action — perhaps Barbox could have saved the signalman if he had informed someone of his mental state.

GLOSSARY

quarter direction

at last set free he'd recently retired from his job

saturnine gloomy

natural philosophy the study of physics based on experiments and data

without outside

fallen colour gone pale

perspective glass an early kind of telescope

A *Identify the speaker.*

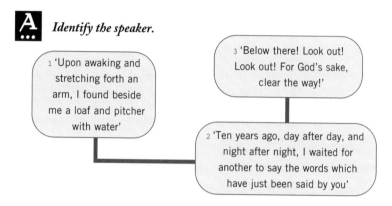

1 'Upon awaking and stretching forth an arm, I found beside me a loaf and pitcher with water'

3 'Below there! Look out! Look out! For God's sake, clear the way!'

2 'Ten years ago, day after day, and night after night, I waited for another to say the words which have just been said by you'

Identify the person or animals 'to whom' these comments refer.

4 Forth from the well they hurried in fresh troops. They clung to the wood – they overran it, and leaped in hundreds upon my person

5 He was a pretty musician, and he would put his flute in his pocket, after office hours, and stroll over to the house, and sit there in the twilight playing to the father and daughter

6 He had been, when young ... a student of natural philosophy, and had attended lectures, but he had run wild

Check your answers on page 93.

B *Consider these issues.*

a The significance of the choice of narrator, and the effect of this on the reader's response.

b The importance of location and setting in creating the mood and atmosphere.

c The relevance of Victorian moral and social values to these stories.

M.R. JAMES

Montague Rhodes James (1862–1936) is arguably the best ghost-story writer Britain has produced. He was the son of an East Anglian clergyman, a brilliant linguist and scholar, and became head of a Cambridge college and Eton public school. He read his terrifying stories aloud to his students by candlelight.

Lost Hearts

In September 1811, Stephen Elliott, an eleven-year-old boy orphaned six months previously, arrives at Aswarby Hall in Lincolnshire to live with his elderly cousin, Mr Abney. Everyone had been surprised when the austere, scholarly Mr Abney had offered Stephen a home. He welcomes Stephen enthusiastically, but seems preoccupied by the boy's exact age.

Stephen soon meets Mrs Bunch, the housekeeper, who tells him about Mr Abney's kindness, eighteen years earlier, in taking in an odd girl, Phoebe, who had mysteriously disappeared after three weeks, and Giovanni, who had also vanished soon after arriving, about eleven years later.

This story includes some grotesque and horrific incidents. Do they enhance or detract from its success?

That night Stephen has a terrifying vision of a body lying in the bath near his bedroom. He wakes to find himself standing outside the bathroom door, but, after bravely checking, finds no body inside.

In March 1812, Stephen wakes from a restless night to find mysterious scratches on his night-gown above his heart, and on the door, and the following night he overhears the butler telling Mrs Bunch about supernatural voices in the wine-cellar.

On the spring equinox, Mr Abney asks Stephen to come to his study secretly at 11 p.m. Stephen notices Mr Abney preparing equipment for an occult ceremony in the library.

Before going to his cousin's study, while standing by his open window, Stephen hears eerie sounds from the nearby woods, and sees the ghostly figures of a boy and girl looking up at him. The girl resembles the figure in his dream, while the boy, who has a black, gaping hole in his left side, is gesturing menacingly.

Stephen is inquiring and brave, but are we more perceptive about the dangers than he is?

Terrified, Stephen enters his cousin's study and finds him dead, with a terrible wound exposing his heart. The window is open and the coroner thinks Abney was killed by a wild animal. However, from his cousin's papers, Stephen learns that Abney had killed Phoebe and Giovanni, and planned to kill him that evening. Abney's studies in the occult had indicated he could gain spiritual powers by absorbing the hearts of three young victims, then disposing of their bodies in a bathroom or wine cellar. Abney hadn't counted on ghostly revenge!

COMMENT

The title of this story contains a rather grim **pun** (see Literary Terms). Abney, Phoebe and Giovanni literally lose their hearts, but, as the heart is traditionally the location of love and feeling, Abney has **metaphorically** (see Literary Terms) lost his too. He has put the selfish pursuit of occult powers before love for others, even when these are innocent children.

Abney, like the legendary Faust, has sold his soul in return for supernatural powers.

Abney is a stereotypical literary figure – a reclusive, austere, cerebral person who loves books more than people. When such a person dabbles in the occult (the story is a warning against doing so) the damage to himself and others is profound. His name is significant, because Mr Abney has abnegated his responsibilities as a human being, scholar and protector of innocent children. This story is partly about the destruction of childhood innocence.

M.R. James provides hints that not all is as it seems. Did you spot that:

- Abney specifically checked Stephen's and Giovanni's ages
- Giovanni and Phoebe are solitary children who wouldn't be missed
- The house has a melancholy atmosphere.

Abney is another man who dismisses the power of ghosts and pays the price.

The one source of comfort is that the supernatural powers do not allow Abney ultimate success. In this story, as in *The Judge's House*, the spirit world is aggressive and vindictive. These are ghosts to be scared of, and, although Abney has no right to our sympathy, we wonder whether we should all be worried if ghosts can act like this.

M.R. James claimed that in ghost stories plot is more important than characterisation. Is it true of this story?

There are several interesting aspects about the way the story has been written:

- Precise architectural detail in the description of the house.
- Many scholarly references to give credibility to a fantastic plot, but not all are genuine – M.R. James was prepared to make up a suitably impressive reference!
- Use of **dialogue** to suggest that Abney may have sinister motives for inviting Stephen (see p. 120), but the **omniscient narrator** (see Literary Terms) then tells us what we should have deduced from it.
- Use of gentle **irony** (see Literary Terms) at the expense of Mrs Bunch. She is garrulous, but M.R. James's criticism is gentle and affectionate when he writes, using **litotes** (see Literary Terms), 'she was by no means disinclined to communicate her information' (p. 121). Can you find a similarly ironic comment in the next paragraph?
- Suspense is maintained by including the extract from Abney's papers before telling us his fate.

GLOSSARY   **post-chaise** a hired, low, open carriage pulled by one or two ponies

Aswarby Aswarby is near Sleaford in Lincolnshire

reign of Queen Anne Anne ruled from 1702 to 1714

cupola a dome

the Mysteries those cults of the ancient world open only to
initiates

the Orphic poems Orphism was an ancient Greek mystery cult
which aimed for immortality. The Orphic hymns (poems)
formed part of the secret rites

the worship of Mithras Mithras was the Persian god of light, and
the power of goodness

Neo-Platonists followers of the religious and philosophical
movement combining the thoughts of the Greek philosopher,
Plato, and oriental mysticism

Levant countries between Greece and Egypt

in fine in short

pore poor

somethink something

Jevanny Giovanni

a tweaking his 'urdy gurdy turning the handle of his barrel-organ

ast asked

hunruly unruly

St Michan's Church the vaults of this church, in Church Street,
Dublin, contain seventeenth-century mummified bodies,
preserved because the limestone walls absorb water

flinders tatters

scorings gashes

Robinson Crusoe novel of 1719 by Daniel Defoe about the
adventures of a shipwrecked man

Simon Magus an early magician who conjured evil spirits to help
him to attempt to fly

Clementine Recognitions religious book attributed to Clementine
the First

Hermes Trismegistus the name given to the Egyptian god, Thoth,
by the neo-Platonists. His name means 'the thrice-great
Hermes'

philosophic temperament calm temperament

THOMAS HARDY

Thomas Hardy was born near Dorchester in 1840. He worked as an architect until his mid-thirties, when he married his first wife, Emma. He wrote novels and stories for the next twenty years, including *Tess of the d'Urbervilles* (1891) and *Jude the Obscure* (1895), but the reaction to the latter was so hostile that he never wrote fiction again, concentrating exclusively on poetry. Thomas Hardy died in 1928 and his heart was buried in Dorset.

The Three Strangers

Notice how the rain is hostile and aggressive. Hardy compares it with arrows, and it 'smote' the walls.

On a wet, windy night in the 1820s, a christening party is taking place in shepherd Fennel's lonely cottage on a Dorset hillside. As the guests dance, a gaunt stranger of about forty, dressed in thick cloth and hobnailed boots, approaches the cottage. The shepherd welcomes him, gives him a drink and tobacco, and he sits by the fire to dry.

Soon, a slightly older, fatter, grey-haired and grey-suited stranger, arrives unexpectedly. He is on his way to Casterbridge, and goes to sit beside the first stranger, who offers him a drink. The grey man tells his hosts that he has to be at work in Casterbridge by 8 a.m.

The conversation turns to occupations and the first stranger claims to be a wheelwright, while the second stranger is initially reluctant to reveal his job. He is a little drunk, and tells the others obliquely, in a song, that he is a hangman on his way to execute someone for sheep-stealing. The guests are shocked, and realise the condemned man is Timothy Summers, who stole a sheep to feed his starving family.

Presently a small, fair, dark-suited stranger arrives. As he is about to ask the way to Casterbridge, he spots the grey man, trembles as he hears the third verse of his song, and rushes out of the house. The tension increases when the sound of gunfire indicates a prisoner has escaped from Casterbridge jail.

The gullible locals are convinced the last stranger is the escaped prisoner, and they give chase, led by an incompetent constable, while the women comfort the crying baby upstairs, leaving the room empty.

Soon the first stranger returns to help himself to cake and a drink. The hangman briefly returns, before they leave in opposite directions, the hangman for Casterbridge.

Meanwhile, after a chaotic pursuit, the posse thinks it has found its quarry under a tree. He makes no protest when he is arrested and taken to the cottage. Here he is confronted by a magistrate and two jailers, who, to general consternation, inform the locals their captive is not the escaped prisoner, whose appearance actually corresponds with the first stranger's.

The captured man tells them he had been walking to Casterbridge to bid a final farewell to the condemned man, his brother, when he called at the cottage. He was so flabbergasted to find him sitting beside his appointed hangman, he dashed out. The real convict disappeared, never to be seen again.

COMMENT Much of this story's interest comes from the author's occasionally ambivalent attitude to the country people, but, even when he is **ironic** (see Literary Terms), he is warm and affectionate. This is apparent in the description of the shepherds on page 132, where Thomas Hardy admires their serenity and lack of worldly ambition.

The hangman bears the weight of the author's disapproval. He patronises the local people, and exploits their innate kindness. Ironically he is a much less attractive character than the man he is going to hang. Note the difference in the way they greet the locals and ask for shelter. The description of the hangman (p. 138) is disapproving. He is an outsider, unable to appreciate the values of rural life.

The incompetent constable, reminiscent of William Shakespeare's Dogberry (in Much Ado About Nothing*), is an equally unimpressive representative of the law.*

The **images** (see Literary Terms) associated with the hangman are almost all negative. He represents a legal system which protects the property of the haves against the have-nots, and the rural community clearly has much sympathy with Timothy Summers. Any just system would not execute him for stealing simply to feed his family.

The opening is typical Thomas Hardy, with the detailed description of a rural landscape at best indifferent to humans, interspersed with philosophical reflections. As usual in Thomas Hardy, when the human approaches, he is seen as tiny against the background landscape.

The story uses the common device of mistaken identity and we are offered a series of conflicting values: e.g. humans versus nature, law versus justice, town versus country, Shepherd Fennel versus his wife, generosity versus meanness.

There is humour at the expense of the rustics, especially the constable and Mrs Fennel's meanness. At the same time there is admiration for country wisdom (note the comments about having babies on p. 136). Thomas Hardy is often gently **ironic** (see Literary Terms): e.g. about Mrs Fennel, 'who brought fifty guineas in her pocket – and kept them there' (p. 132) and frequently uses **litotes** (see Literary Terms) to achieve this: e.g. 'sounds of not unmixed purity of tone' (p. 133); 'thoughts not of the gayest kind' (p. 143); 'not unwelcome diversion' (p. 136); 'not unprepossessing as to feature' (p. 136).

This story has been criticised for relying too heavily on a series of coincidences. Do you agree that it does?

As in many mystery stories we are given clues to solve the conundrum. These are some indications that the first stranger is the prisoner:
- He takes a long drink of water before going in
- He has a quick look around the room and checks he isn't being pursued
- He has no pipe, tobacco or tin
- He hides in the chimney corner
- He deflects questions about his home by flattering the questioner

Did you spot others?

GLOSSARY

furzy covered in furze (gorse)

coombs valleys set in hillsides

ewe-leases sheep meadows

hard by near by

clothyard shafts of Senlac and Crecy arrows one-yard long used at the battles of Hastings (Senlac Hill) (1066) and Crecy (1346)

calling occupation

back-brand a large burning log at the back of the fire

'like the laughter of the fool' a quotation from Ecclesiastes in the Bible

pourparlers informal discussions

fifty guineas £52.50p, roughly the equivalent of two years' wages

tweedledee sound of a violin

groundbass often-repeated bass passage, like a bass 'riff'

serpent obsolete wooden wind instrument

crownpiece a coin worth five shillings (25p)

apogee to perigee from that point in a planet's orbit when it is
    furthest from the earth to that point when it is nearest to the
    earth

pent-roof a sloping roof of a subsidiary structure joined to a
    main building

meads meadows near a river

bleared blurred

vamp sole of a shoe

brands sticks or logs

grog-blossoms pimples or redness on the nose from drinking
    alcohol

fob small pocket in waistband of breeches for keeping a watch
    etc

Casterbridge Dorchester

Shottsford Blandford

mead / small mead alcoholic drink made from honey. Small
    mead is weaker

metheglin spiced mead

comb-washings washing out the honeycombs to harvest the last
    vestiges of honey. This would produce a weaker drink

het or wet hot or wet

Daze it Dash it

bee-burning smoking the bees out of the hives so that the honey
    could be collected

Belshazzar's Feast the feast of Belshazzar, the son of
    Nebuchadnezzar, at which his doom was foretold by writing on
    the wall

jiggered confounded

zeed saw (past tense of 'see')

yaller yellow

lion and unicorn the symbol of the Crown's power

hurdle rectangular wooden frame for making temporary fences

skimmer cake cake baked on a skimming ladle

cretaceous chalky
culpet culprit
preternatural supernatural
turnkey jailer
benighted overtaken by night
raze erase
hob and nobbing hob-nobbing; mixing with
sere and yellow leaf old age

BRAM STOKER

Abraham (Bram) Stoker was born in Dublin in 1847. After graduating in science from Trinity College, Dublin. He worked as a civil servant, before becoming, for twenty-seven years, the manager of the great Victorian actor, Sir Henry Irving. He wrote many horror stories in the 1880s, including one, *The Squaw*, in which the avenging spirit returns as a cat. His only successful novel was the famous *Dracula* (1897). He died in 1912.

The Judge's House

Wishing to have peace to prepare for his university Mathematics examination, Malcolm Malcolmson rents an old, rambling, Jacobean house in Benchurch, where he is unknown. This shocks the landlady of the inn because the house, which used to belong to a cruel judge, has been unoccupied because it has 'something strange' about it.

As Malcolmson explores the large dining room where he plans to study, he sees and hears rats, and notices a thick rope hanging by the fireplace.

Malcolmson spends his first night there studying, but, close to dawn, he is shocked to see a giant rat sitting on a large chair, glaring at him. He has to chase it with a poker before it escapes up the rope by the fireplace.

When he settles to work the following evening, the rats are noisier. He becomes aware, at about midnight, that

*What are the effects
on the reader of
the fairly detailed
description of Mrs
Witham exploring
the house on pages
156 and 157?*

it has gone quiet, and he sees the giant rat again glaring at him from the big chair. He drives the rat up the rope and decides to find its lair. After its next visit, he sees it disappear through a hole into one of the huge pictures on the wall.

When he is out the following day, Malcolmson meets a local doctor who, when he tells him about the rat, informs Malcolm the rope was used by the hangman to execute prisoners sentenced by the cruel judge.

That night Malcolmson tries to study, but is too fascinated by the rope's history. He inspects the picture into which the rat escapes, and is stunned to find it is a portrait of the judge, whose glaring eyes are a replica of the rat's, sitting in the high-backed chair in the room. When he turns, the rat is sitting in the high-backed chair.

About an hour later, with a storm raging outside, he is disturbed by the rat gnawing through the rope, which falls to the floor, meaning Malcolm cannot ring the alarm bell for help. He notices the judge has disappeared from the picture, and, as Malcolm turns, he sees him sitting in the chair donning his black cap. Outside, the clock strikes midnight.

The judge grabs the rope from the floor, makes a noose, and attempts to throw it around the student's neck. For some time Malcolmson manages to dodge. Hordes of rats pour down the rope and their weight makes the alarm bell ring. The judge is angry that Malcolm may be rescued after all, and puts the noose around the student's neck. He attaches the noose to the bell rope and hangs Malcolmson.

Aroused by the bell, some villagers burst in to find Malcolmson hanged, and a malignant smile on the face of the judge in the picture.

COMMENT   This story is deeply **symbolic** (see Literary Terms). The
judge/rat is a symbol of the power of evil in the
universe. Both Malcolmson and Mrs Witham refer
to the rat as 'The old devil' in their conversation on
page 161.

Malcolmson is able to drive the rat away only when
he hits it with the Bible, while his mathematical
textbooks are useless. The message is clear. Science,
logic and rationality cannot combat the power of Satan.
All that can is the word of God, which contradicts
those who were sceptical of the Bible's value in a
scientific age.

*Malcolmson shows
the arrogance of
youth in contrast
with the wisdom
of age.*

Once more a young man ignores the advice of the
unsophisticated locals, who may lack his intellectual
powers, but respect the supernatural. Malcolmson
arrogantly comments that a mathematics student has
'too much to think of to be disturbed by any of these
mysterious "somethings"' (p. 156).

*Malcolmson is
consistently
sceptical,
dismissive and
ironic about the
supernatural.*

His rational mind gives him no power to overcome evil,
for the judge exacts the ultimate penalty on
Malcolmson for ignoring the advice of Mrs Witham
and Dr Thorndike. The instinct of the locals to respect
the supernatural is more useful than any academic
knowledge.

There is criticism of the dedicated intellectual who puts
the pursuit of knowledge before human relationships.
Malcolmson's enthusiasm for study is impressive. He
views another long period of study 'with joy', and
becomes so absorbed in abstract mathematical problems
that he is oblivious to everything else.

There is an interesting contrast between the views of
Mrs Dempster and Mrs Witham on the supernatural.
The former confidently states that bogeys are mere
figments of the imagination, with rational
explanations, but we see that this intellectual position

does not make her any less reluctant to be alone in the judge's house!

Note how Malcolmson inverts the natural order by working at night and sleeping during the day.

Malcolmson rejection of society is dangerous. A recurring **theme** (see Literary Terms) in the stories is the danger of self-imposed solitude, and Bram Stoker stresses that Malcolmson prefers his own company. He soon learns the error of his ways at the end of a rope. The two women and Dr Thornhill show the human concern which Malcolmson needs.

Bram Stoker suggests the other rats are the judge's victims too. He probably terrorises them, and they quieten only when he leaves the wall. The ordinary rats try to save Malcolmson by weighing down the rope so that the bell rings to summon help, which sadly comes just too late. They see him as a fellow-victim, and they want to destroy their oppressor.

GLOSSARY

Jacobean style the style of James the First's reign (1603–25)
rarely to an unusual degree
Assizes courts held in each county by High Court judges
Mathematical Tripos the examination for a Mathematics degree at Cambridge University
Harmonical Progression; Permutations and Combinations; and Elliptic Functions these are all mathematical subjects
his commissions his instructions
mayhap possibly
incontinently uncontrollably
wainscoting wooden panelling on lower part of wall
Senior Wrangler the person who gained the highest mark in the Mathematical Tripos
Greenhow's Charity this was presumably the name of a local charity which provided houses for the poor. There were often strict residency rules
Saint Anthony the founder of Christian Monasticism who overcame many worldly temptations
sang froid calm composure

Laplace Pierre Simon, Marquis de Laplace, (1749–1827)
developed probability theory and wrote a textbook on celestial
mechanics
Conic Sections, Cycloidal Oscillations, Principia, Quaternians and
Thermodynamics these are mathematics textbooks
black cap a judge would don a black cap when sentencing
someone to death. The italic text emphasises Malcolmson's
horror
running noose a noose with a knot which tightens as the rope is
pulled

Ambrose bierce

Ambrose Bierce (1842–1914) was born in Ohio, and
fought with some distinction in the American Civil
War before spending much of his life as a journalist,
poet and short-story writer. He lived in England from
1872–6. Ambrose Bierce's death is shrouded in mystery,
but he was probably shot in Mexico in 1914.

An
Occurrence at
Owl Creek
Bridge

Peyton Farquhar, a rich plantation owner from
Alabama, regrets he is unable fight in the Civil War,
and does all he can to support the Southern cause.

Some time before the story begins, a disguised enemy
scout had visited Farquhar's house on a pretext and told
him the Federal forces had captured the bridge at Owl
Creek, about thirty miles away and had issued an edict
that anyone caught interfering with the railroad and its

Note how in the
first section
Farquhar is not
named, but is 'a
man' or 'the man'.

bridges would be hanged. The soldier had also revealed
that lots of dried, flammable driftwood was trapped
behind the bridge. Acting on this information,
Farquhar had attempted to sabotage the bridge, and
had been captured.

When the story opens, Farquhar is standing on one end
of the bridge, with his hands tied behind his back and a
noose around his neck, waiting to be hanged. He looks

*What is the effect
of the description
of the soldiers, and
the use of military
terms, in the first
two paragraphs of
the story?*

at the stream below, closes his eyes and tries to fix his
last thoughts on his family. He imagines being able to
throw off the noose, evade the bullets and swim for
safety. At that moment the sergeant steps off the plank
which had supported Farquhar's feet.

Farquhar imagines he has freed his hands and swum to
the surface. He seems intensely alive to the details and
beauty of the natural world. He thinks he is dreaming,
and sees distorted soldiers on the bridge, gesticulating
and shouting at him.

Suddenly he hears a bullet, fired from the bridge,
striking the water near him. Farquhar hears the captain
ordering the whole company to fire, and decides to dive
as deep as possible. As he surfaces, he encounters a
fusillade of bullets, and is hit in the neck. He drifts
further from the bridge and swims with the current. A
huge splash nearby indicates a cannon has been fired at
him, again missing.

Suddenly Farquhar is caught in a whirlpool, and
deposited on some gravel on the southern shore, out of
sight of his enemy. He is overjoyed. A volley of
grapeshot stirs him from his dream and he plunges into
the forest.

Farquhar travels through the apparently impenetrable forest all day, until he finds a road leading towards his home. As he walks along, the forest and sky look unreal, his neck hurts, he can't close his congested eye and his tongue is frozen.

He imagines falling asleep and dreams that he is at the gate of his home. Farquhar walks up the path and his wife, looking fresh, cool and sweet, steps down from the veranda to meet him. He springs forward to her with extended arms. As he is about to clasp her, he feels a stunning blow on the back of the neck, a blazing white light, then darkness and silence. He has been executed.

COMMENT

Details in the story are strikingly similar to those given by people who have 'died' and been resuscitated.

This story's claim to success lies in its technical innovations. These include:

- Ambrose Bierce builds a whole short story around the last seconds of a man's life.
- We think the events are actually happening, but we are being given a detailed account of the imaginings of a mind starved of oxygen, in the last seconds of its existence.
- One of the most impressive things is the **'twist in the tail'** (see Literary Terms), when we are told Farquhar is dead at the moment we thought he was safely home.
- Ambrose Bierce has cleverly manipulated the chronology (natural time sequence) and described the scene on the bridge before the visit of the scout which triggered the action. This flashback technique, although commonplace now, was unusual in the nineteenth century.
- The account of being under fire is dramatic and immediate. We are caught up in the drama of the apparent escape.

There is an inevitability about Farquhar's actions, for he lived within the confines of a strict code of honour as a Southern gentleman. He may well have felt the need to prove his bravery and devotion to the Southern cause, which the scout is able to exploit by planting an idea in his mind, showing that other armies and cultures achieve their ends by more devious means than a southern gentleman would.

Note Ambrose Bierce's clipped journalistic style, with one-clause sentences, especially in the opening.

There is a strong photographic feel to the scene on the bridge, with fixity and lack of movement achieved by repetition of words such as 'statue', 'stonily', 'motionless' and 'still'. Technical details give an authentic flavour to the writing.

The characters in Ambrose Bierce's stories often lack individual identity, acting merely as representative, suffering humans. Death is downplayed. The title speaks merely of an 'occurrence', and the execution is an emotionless ritual.

GLOSSARY

hammer apparatus for exploding the charge in a gun

acclivity upward slope

embrasure opening for a gun in a parapet

fixity fixed state

habit clothes

frock coat military, long-skirted coat

hemp rope (made from the hemp plant)

crossties planks going side-to-side across the bridge

circumstances of an imperious nature urgent business

fall of Corinth at the Battle of Corinth, in October 1862, the Federal troops defeated the Confederate army

The Yanks the northern Federal troops

picket post a group of sentries

lines of ramification branches

ramrods rods for ramming down the charge of a muzzle loaded firearm

diminuendo gradual decrease of loudness

grape small balls as a scattering charge for.cannon

aeolian harps harps suspended from trees so that the wind blowing over the strings creates a melody

Identify the speaker.

1 'Gracious me, Master Stephen.' ... 'how do you manage to tear your night-dress all to flinders this way?'

2 'My fingers be as full of thorns as an old pincushion is of pins'

4 'I observed that the flood of last winter had lodged a great quantity of driftwood against the wooden pier at this end of the bridge'

3 'It may be that he is in an overwrought state, and has been studying too much, although I am bound to say that he seems as sound and healthy a young man, mentally and bodily, as ever I saw'

Identify the persons 'to whom' these comments refer.

5 In his left side was a terrible lacerated wound, exposing the heart

6 He appeared tall, but a recruiting sergeant, or other person accustomed to the judging of men's heights by the eye, would have discerned that this was chiefly owing to his gauntness

8 His features were good – a straight nose, firm mouth, broad forehead, from which his long, dark hair was combed straight back, falling behind his ears to the collar of his well-fitting frock coat

7 His face was strong and merciless, evil, crafty and vindictive, with a sensual mouth, hooked nose of ruddy colour, and shaped like the beak of a bird of prey

Check your answers on page 93.

 Consider these issues.

a The difference in the descriptive style of Ambrose Bierce and Thomas Hardy in the first couple of pages of their stories.

b The importance of dialogue in these stories.

c The effectiveness of the conclusions to the stories.

d The similarities and differences between the servants in *The Judge's House* and *Lost Hearts*.

AMELIA B. EDWARDS

Amelia B. Edwards was born in London in 1831, and started writing at an early age, partly to help with the family's financial difficulties. She specialised in writing ghost stories for magazines, but had several novels published in the 1860s. She travelled to Egypt in 1873, and became a leading Egyptologist of her day, and a keen supporter of the movement for female suffrage. She died in 1892.

The Phantom Coach

What impression do you gain of James Murray, especially from his conversation with the scientist on pages 188 and 189?

The narrator, James Murray, a barrister, describes what happened to him twenty years earlier. After spending a cold December day grouse-shooting on a bleak Northern moor, as evening falls with an icy wind and the first flakes of a snow-storm, he realises he is lost. He has to seek shelter, for he is weary and hungry.

As the snow falls more heavily, he thinks of his wife, waiting at home for his promised return before dusk. As he walks through the deepening darkness, his shouts for help are answered, and he sees the light of a lantern. It is Jacob, who tells him he is twenty miles from his home village, and twelve miles from the nearest one. Jacob is unfriendly, and tells James his master won't invite him in to shelter.

They arrive at the house and go into a cluttered hall with a large telescope in the middle. James is summoned to the master's room, where a 'huge, white-haired old man rose from a table covered with books and papers' (p. 188). His study looks incongruous in a farmhouse because it is full of books and scientific instruments.

Reluctantly, the owner offers James shelter and food. After a plain dinner, the host says he has lived in strict retirement from the world for twenty-three years, and that James is the first stranger he has seen for four years. He asks James to tell him of the world and modern scientific progress, and speaks to him, knowledgeably and impressively, of many subjects.

The host speaks about supernatural matters, and bitterly criticises modern scientists for scorning those with faith in the supernatural. He had been forced to retire to the isolated farmhouse because of ridicule by his scientific peers.

When James explains his anxiety to return immediately to his wife, the owner tells him there is a night mail-coach which will pass about five miles from the house in an hour and a quarter.

James sets off with Jacob as his taciturn guide, but is left to walk the last three miles alone along the old coach road. Jacob warns him to take care near a signpost where the parapet remains broken after a fatal accident nine years earlier, when a coach plunged over the edge, killing six people.

As a breathless James is resting against a stone wall, he is delighted to see the lights of an approaching coach, though surprised to see it on the dangerous old coach-road.

There are three male passengers in the coach, which is cold and smells unpleasant. James elicits no response when he tries to engage his fellow travellers in conversation. When he opens the window, he notices the whole coach is dilapidated.

Does the scientist deliberately put Murray in the path of the phantoms by directing him to the old coach-road?

When a passenger turns towards him, James notices he is a ghost, and the others are also phantoms. As he desperately tries to jump out, the phantom coach plunges off the road exactly where the fatal accident occurred nine years earlier.

When he recovers consciousness at home, his wife tells him he fell over a precipice near the site of the fatal coach crash, and was lucky to escape death because he landed in a deep snow-drift. He had sustained a fractured skull and broken arm. Shepherds had found him and his wife had nursed him back to health. James is convinced he has been a passenger in a phantom coach, but his surgeon is more sceptical.

COMMENT

The author tries to give the narrator credibility – he's middle class with a barrister's mentality. Does he convince you?

This story includes a categorical statement of faith in the supernatural but we do not necessarily believe it. As it is a **first person narrator** (see Literary Terms) we have only Murray's view. It is possible to believe Murray's experience is entirely imagined as he stumbles along affected by the cold, the alcohol and recently-heard stories of the supernatural. The first sentence attempts to deflect such a view by stating the story is 'the truth'.

The retired scientist is an important figure, who attacks the prevailing attitude of Victorian scientists. He concludes, 'They condemn as fable all that resists experiment' (pp. 191–2).

This is a conventional ghost story, in a typically isolated setting, but the characters of the scientist and Jacob, plus the vivid description of the coach and ghosts, provide interest.

GLOSSARY

smoke-wreath a curl of smoke

fain willing

speculum mirror of polished metal in a reflecting telescope

galvanic battery a primary battery for producing electrical current

idealists philosophers who believe knowledge depends on the activity of the brain rather than any objective reality

Louis von Beethoven presumably the author means Ludwig von Beethoven, the composer

viands pieces of food

Watts the author probably means James Watt (1736–1819), the Scottish engineer

Mesmer Anton Mesmer (1733–1815) Austrian physician and early exponent of hypnotism

Reichenbach Georg von Reichenbach (1772–1826) maker of telescopes and other astronomical apparatus

Swedenborg Emmanuel Swedenborg (1688–1772) Swedish scientist, theologian and philosopher

Spinoza Benedict Spinoza (1632–77) Dutch philosopher

Condillac Etienne Bonnot de Condillac (1715–80) philosopher and psychologist

Descartes Rene Descartes (1596–1650) influential French philosopher and mathematician

Berkeley George Berkeley (1685–1753) Anglo-Irish bishop, philosopher and scientist

Aristotle (384–322BC) Greek philosopher, student of Plato

Plato (429–347BC) Greek philosopher, pupil of Socrates and teacher of Aristotle

Magi Three Wise Men

Pagan people who don't believe in any of the main world religions

Pantheist people who believe that God is present throughout, and identical to, Nature

Materialists people who believe that only the material world exists – excludes a concept of God or gods

usquebaugh whisky

comforters woollen scarves

GUY DE MAUPASSANT

Guy de Maupassant was born in Normandy, France in 1850. He studied law and did military service before working as a clerk in the Naval Ministry. He wrote over three hundred stories, mainly for newspapers. He died prematurely in 1893, after a period of insanity.

A Vendetta   The widow Saverini, her son, Antoine, and their dog, Frisky, live overlooking Bonifacio, in Corsica. One night Antoine is murdered by Nicolas Ravolati, who immediately escapes across the narrow strait to Sardinia, and the apparent safety of a different country.

As she and the dog keep a night's vigil by his body, Antoine's mother promises her dead son he will be avenged. It is a matter of honour in Corsica that a victim's family must avenge the death, but Antoine has no close male relative to do this.

Every day the dog howls while the widow stares across the narrow strip of water to the Sardinian village where she knows Nicolas has taken refuge with Corsican bandits. As she is a frail old woman, she doesn't know how she can gain revenge, but she knows she must keep her promise to her dead son.

What is Maupassant implying when he writes that the widow had the 'Fierce vindictive inspiration of a savage'?

One night, she has a flash of inspiration. The following morning she goes to church to pray for God's help. She chains the dog up, starves her for a couple of days, and stuffs some of her late husband's clothes with hay to make a life-like dummy, which she attaches to a stake in front of the dog kennel.

Next she buys a long sausage, which she grills near the kennel, so that the starving Frisky is maddened by the aroma of cooking meat. She ties the sausage around the neck of the dummy, then releases the starving Frisky, who tears its throat and face to pieces in her frenzy to eat.

For three months she makes the dog go through this routine to obtain food, and trains the dog to attack the dummy at her command. A successful attack is rewarded with some meat.

At last it is time to put her plan into action. She goes to confession and takes communion, disguises herself as an old beggar man, and arranges for a fisherman to take her and Frisky across to Sardinia. Frisky hasn't been fed for two days, and Madame Saverini repeatedly allows her to sniff the sausage in her basket to whet her appetite.

When they arrive, Madame Saverini finds Nicolas's house and sets Frisky on him. The dog tears out his throat. Neighbours later report having seen an old beggar feeding an emaciated dog outside the house. The widow Saverini returns home, and sleeps soundly, having fulfilled her promise to her dead son.

COMMENT   The opening is crucial in conveying the values of the society. Its detachment from the outside world of civilisation is stressed, and the sea and the elements are as violent and destructive as the widow. The houses look like 'nests of wild birds' above a 'dangerous channel, into which few ships venture' (p. 200). The wind 'harasses the sea remorselessly' and 'roars down the strait, stripping the land bare' (p. 200).

Although generally detached and unemotional, there is horrific detail: e.g. the 'clots of dried blood on his beard and hair' (p. 201).

We are struck by the story's spare and direct style, in contrast with much Victorian writing. It reads like a newspaper report, written by a detached and indifferent observer, intent on reporting facts, without comment. This is remarkable when we remember the intensity of the emotions and the violence of the actions.

The setting of this story is crucial. Mediterranean countries have always had a strict code of honour, including the concept of vendetta. It is an expression of natural justice, and hence older than any legal system. Legally, Nicolas is safe because he has escaped beyond Corsican jurisdiction to another country, but the quest for justice by an aggrieved mother accepts no such artificial boundaries. She must have been especially enraged that Nicolas was living so close, but safe because of an accident of history.

If the contrast between justice and legality is a central **theme** (see Literary Terms), so is the clash between Old and New Testament values. Although the widow invokes the help of God, and attends church before she does the act, her principle is the Old Testament one of 'an eye for an eye'. There is none of the New Testament concept of forgiveness and loving enemies.

The widow has had to adopt a traditionally masculine role, in initiating and planning this gruesomely-violent act. It is no accident that she disguises herself as a man, because she has had to suppress the traditional feminine virtues and adopt traditionally aggressive masculine ones.

Nicolas has broken codes of honour by killing 'treacherously' and hiding from justice. There is a strong sense of inevitability about the action. Nicolas sets in motion events which can be resolved only by his death. This satisfies the reader's and the society's sense of justice and just retribution, as is the case in classic **tragedy** (see Literary Terms).

It is also a story about the depth of maternal love, and about keeping faith with loved ones. It is significant that she is a widow, who seems to have focused all her love on her son.

The plot and themes are crucial in this story. There is very little **dialogue** (see Literary Terms) or attempt to develop the characters. It is a timeless universal issue, so individual identity is unimportant.

GLOSSARY   **vendetta** any prolonged feud, in particular the practice that existed until recently in Corsica, Sardinia and Sicily, of exacting revenge for the murder of a relative by killing a member of the murderer's family

Ajaccio the capital of Corsica

raw-boned gaunt

gun-dog a dog trained to retrieve shot game-birds

maquis vegetation common in Mediterranean countries

black blood-sausage 'black pudding' made from animal blood and suet

H.G. WELLS

Herbert George Wells was born in 1866. His father was a professional cricketer, but the family was poor, and H.G. Wells had to leave school to be an apprentice draper. Scholarships enabled him to take a science degree at London University. He turned to writing when tuberculosis forced him to abandon teaching. H.G. Wells is best known for his science fiction novels, including *The Time Machine* (1895) and *The War of the Worlds* (1898), but he was a prolific writer. He died in 1946.

The Red Room

The narrator plans to spend the night in the allegedly haunted red room of Lorraine Castle. The elderly servants looking after the house counsel him against this. Despite claiming to have an open mind about ghosts, he is sceptical, and critical of elderly people, whom he finds physically repulsive.

On the way up to the red room, he consoles himself that its reputation owes much to the original incident, when a resident's attempt to play a joke on his timid wife had tragic results. The most recent inhabitant, a

young duke, had fallen down the stairs next to the red
room, but the narrator is convinced he died of apoplexy
rather than supernatural causes.

You may like to
compare this story
with the famous
account of Jane
being locked in the
frightening red
room at Gateshead
Hall in Chapter 2
of Jane Eyre *by*
Charlotte Brontë.

He enters the red room, locks himself in, and explores
windows, chimney and panelling, but finds nothing
untoward. He closes the shutters, lights the fire and all
the candles, and sits at the table, placing his revolver on
it.

To ease his self-confessed nervousness, he composes
and recites aloud poems about the castle's legends, but
he is frightened by echoes of his voice. The candles and
fire are flickering in the draughts, which creates
shadows, so he fetches more candles from the landing.

After midnight, the candle in the alcove goes out,
followed by two other candles, and then all the rest. He
rushes around trying to relight them. Panicking, he
bruises himself against the table, knocks a chair
headlong, falls and drags the cloth from the table.

Eventually only the glow from the fire remains. He
hopes he can light the candles from it, but the fire goes
out too. He screams and runs for the door, but cannot
find his way there. He bangs the side of the bed,
staggers up, and either strikes or is struck by a piece of

bulky furniture. He feels a heavy blow on his forehead, a sensation of falling, and then nothing.

He awakes in daylight with a roughly-bandaged head. The servants tell him they found him at dawn, with blood on his forehead and lips. When they ask him which ghost haunts the red room, he answers, 'Fear!'.

COMMENT   This story provides an apt conclusion to the collection because it suggests that phenomena some people call supernatural are the product of a vivid imagination and fear. It is this emotion that haunts the visitors to the red room, so that sinister forces are imagined for events which have a purely natural explanation. Alternatively, someone may see something clearly, but it has no objective existence outside the person's mind.

We again meet an arrogant young man who says at the beginning, 'it will take a very tangible ghost to frighten me'. Ironically he is quivering in fear a few hours later simply because some candles have gone out!

One manifestation of his arrogance is his dismissive attitude to the elderly servants and comments about senility. He shows disdain for their age and wisdom. As the old woman says, 'There's a many things to see when one's still but eight-and-twenty'. The narrator scorns the old people for belonging to an earlier age when belief in the supernatural was warranted.

How does the use of a first person narrator help to make this story frightening? What is the effect of the imagery on you?   The servants are vivid creations. H.G. Wells emphasises their deformities, exaggerated in the distorted images on the wall. It is a story full of frightening shadows. The servants increase the tension by their chorus of warnings about not going to the red room 'this night of all nights', and our imagination does the rest.

The narrator's walk up the passage conveys the terror created by shadows of statues in the moonlight and

candlelight. H.G. Wells expresses the experience of fear
by powerful imagery. The candle 'left an ocean of
mystery and suggestion beyond its island of light'
(p. 209), and the shadows in the red room creep on
him 'like a ragged stormcloud sweeping out the stars'
(p. 212).

GLOSSARY   **atavistic** reversion to an earlier form

foregathered assembled

sconces wall brackets to hold candlesticks

Ganymede and Eagle in Greek mythology, Ganymede was a
handsome young man snatched by the god Zeus disguised as
an eagle

buhl brass, gold or metal inlaid into wood or tortoise shell

apoplexy a stroke

valances short curtains around the bed frame

Ingoldsby fashion Reverend Richard Harris Barham wrote *The
Ingoldsby Legends* (1840) which mock legends

penumbra partial shadow around an area of deep shadow

A

Identify the speaker.

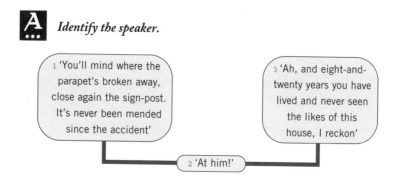

1 'You'll mind where the parapet's broken away, close again the sign-post. It's never been mended since the accident'

3 'Ah, and eight-and-twenty years you have lived and never seen the likes of this house, I reckon'

2 'At him!'

Identify the person(s) 'to whom' this comment refers.

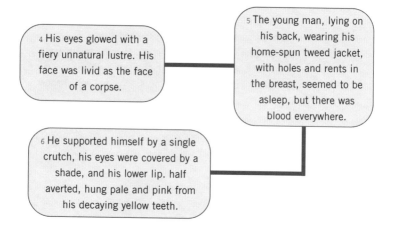

4 His eyes glowed with a fiery unnatural lustre. His face was livid as the face of a corpse.

5 The young man, lying on his back, wearing his home-spun tweed jacket, with holes and rents in the breast, seemed to be asleep, but there was blood everywhere.

6 He supported himself by a single crutch, his eyes were covered by a shade, and his lower lip. half averted, hung pale and pink from his decaying yellow teeth.

Check your answers on page 93.

B *Consider these issues.*

a The significance of the scientist in *The Phantom Coach.*

b The differences in style between Guy de Maupassant and Amelia B. Edwards.

c The methods H.G. Wells uses to create and maintain tension.

PART THREE

COMMENTARY

THEMES

THE SUPERNATURAL

Are there ghosts?

A **theme** (see Literary Terms) of several of the stories was an issue of critical importance to Victorians. Given the increase in scepticism about the truth of the Bible and Christian theology, and the advancement in scientific understanding, many Victorians wondered if it was possible any longer to believe in any existence beyond this earthly one. If not, then the traditional belief in ghosts, spirits and the supernatural was false, and there had to be natural explanations for 'supernatural' events.

It is interesting to note that there always seems to be a reason for the presence of a ghost. Rarely does it seem a random or inexplicable event.

Several of the stories engage in this debate. At one end of the spectrum, in *The Old Nurse's Story, Lost Hearts* and *The Judge's House*, it seems dead people can return in physical form, acting much as human beings. The spirits of Maude's daughter, the Judge, Phoebe and Giovanni assume their human forms again, and function as humans, though with additional superhuman powers. They leave proof, by acts of destruction and death, that they have returned to this world, and are observed by more than one person, giving some evidence of an objective existence.

Elizabeth Gaskell, the author of *The Old Nurse's Story*, insisted, despite considerable opposition from Charles Dickens, her editor, that the ghostly **dénouement** (see Literary Terms) should be seen by several characters, and not just Rosamond. Readers could not, then, dismiss the ghosts as mere figments of Rosamond's imagination.

Several phantoms are seen by just one person, and, in these cases, authors are much more tentative about whether they are 'real' ghosts or products of a disturbed mind.

Do you think ghosts are figments of the imagination?

For instance, only the signalman sees the ghost and hears the bell. When the narrator is talking to the signalman at the time of the supposed visitation, he sees and hears nothing untoward. It is perfectly feasible that this ghost is a figment of the signalman's imagination and overwrought brain.

James Murray is convinced he sees the phantom coach, but the author provides no corroborative evidence. Murray may have imagined the whole thing, given the events which had preceded his experience.

H.G. Wells's hero is much more confident. There is nothing haunting the red room except fear itself. We are reminded of the words of American President Franklin Roosevelt, 'the only thing to fear is fear itself', when the narrator emerges to proclaim the room is haunted by fear. This story's contribution to the debate is important, for it suggests that supernatural events are the product of imagination and fear, with no objective reality.

Gender and class differences

Attitude to the supernatural varies according to age, class, gender, educational experience and environment. The young, middle-class, well-educated, urban men are much more sceptical than the rural, female servants. Women and children are particularly sensitive to the supernatural, as are servants, who seem aware of strange happenings long before their employers. Servants with this ability include Hester, Dorothy and Bessy in *The Old Nurse's Story*; Mrs Bunch and Mr Parkes in *Lost Hearts*; and Mrs Witham and Mrs Dempster (in spite of what she says, she fears the supernatural) in *The Judge's House*.

The men in these stories are often intellectual and rational, whereas the women, and especially country women, are closer to the spiritual and emotional life, of which ghosts seem a part. Often an arrogant man is forced to amend his view of ghosts, if he is still alive to do so! Both Malcolm Malcolmson and Mr Abney pay with their lives for their conceited denial of the power of ghosts.

The danger of isolation

One of the most dangerous things people can do is to isolate themselves. Not only do ghostly visitations often occur in lonely places, but deliberate withdrawal from others removes human support and love which can counteract the darker supernatural forces. For the signalman and Malcolmson, voluntary withdrawal from the world results in death. Significantly, before Malcolmson dies, the Judge severs the rope which would have enabled him to contact others. Several of the other characters, including Mr Abney, are reclusive, confirming that cutting oneself off from the redeeming power of human love and compassion is dangerous.

The power of love

In contrast, Rosamond survives a potentially fatal encounter with the supernatural because she has Hester's love to protect her. Hester physically and symbolically wrestles Rosamond out of the phantom's grip. Several stories imply there is a moral duty to show love and compassion, as Hester does, when someone is threatened by evil forces. Even the signalman may have been saved if the narrator had acted with greater urgency and removed him from his vulnerable situation.

Supernatural variety

It would be a mistake to suggest that the supernatural is always hostile to the living. Sometimes it simply offers a glimpse into the future, as in Isaac Scatchard's premonitory vision.

However, several of the spirits are vengeful, intent on righting perceived injustices in this world. This is the

case in *The Old Nurse's Story* and *Lost Hearts*, whereas
the Judge seems malevolently disposed to Malcolmson
simply because he has invaded his domain and thrown
books at him.

REVENGE

The thirst for revenge has been a theme in literature
since the earliest Greek plays. Three of the stories are
about the strength of this emotion, and the lengths to
which it drives people. The apparently frail and sickly
widow Saverini is driven to an act of extreme ferocity by
the strength of her desire to avenge her son's death.
Grace Furnivall is prepared to countenance the ruin of
her sister and niece because of jealousy and the wish for
revenge. In return, Grace has to suffer the revenge of
her sister from beyond the grave. Jealousy and revenge
are linked in the case of Samuel Lowgood. He is driven
to underhand and destructive actions, and the sacrifice
of his life savings, by his thirst for revenge.

GENDER ISSUES

The position of women is the most interesting of the
several social and cultural themes raised. The model of
passive, long-suffering Victorian womanhood is Lucy
Malden, who retains her love for the caddish
Christopher Weldon even when he humiliates and
rejects her. She hides the cheque, her husband's only
weapon to discredit Christopher, and, although she
argues this was done to save Samuel from sin, a more
likely reason is to protect the undeserving Christopher.
She condemns herself to unhappiness by marrying,
almost by default, a man she doesn't love, and her own
feelings seem to count for nothing. She is generally
passive and rather insipid, a common type in Victorian
fiction.

However, she acts decisively to save Christopher, and, in so doing, demonstrates the strength of her love.

Somewhat threateningly for the Victorian readership, in doing so she shows that romantic love can be much more powerful than marital bonds.

Think about the presentation of women in the stories. Do the writers generally seem to approve of those who follow the stereotype of femininity and condemn those who don't?

Isaac Scatchard's mother presents a slightly different vision of womanhood, because she is more powerful and resourceful than the man she looks after. However, Isaac's mental limitations are stressed more than his mother's strengths and resourcefulness. When a woman is powerful and assertive, as Rebecca Scatchard is, she is seen as destructive, dangerous and threatening to men.

Most of the other women in the stories are domestic servants, one of the few careers open to them. Women are shown in subservient roles to men. One of the attractions of ghost stories to women must have been that all-powerful, assertive males are reduced to gibbering shadows of their former selves by the supernatural visitors. They exhibit behaviour which they would previously have slightingly characterised as 'typically feminine'.

The perils of patriarchy

The Old Nurse's Story condemns Victorian patriarchy, which gave the father power to decide his family's fate. Maude is unable openly to marry the man she loves, or have her own child to live with her, because her father would disapprove, and his power is absolute. He is prepared to enforce this even when it means casting out his daughter and her child on a bitter night. Total obedience to the patriarch's wishes is essential, even for an upper-class woman.

CLASS

Self-improvement

While Victorian society paid lip-service to the possibilities of self-improvement through thrift and hard work, the reality was different. Samuel Lowgood does all he can to improve himself after a deprived childhood, but he is doomed. The injustice of the class system means that a less able, less hard-working and incompetent person like Christopher Weldon can rise to be a partner because of his connections, appearance and family. This restrained but powerful attack on the class system remains relevant today.

Upper-class failings

The upper classes are strongly criticised in the stories. Several hint at dark secrets behind the doors of the large houses of the most outwardly respectable people. The aristocratic Furnivall family is divided, and has guilty secrets of betrayal, illicit passion, dark emotions and violence. The owner of Aswarby Hall is a child abductor, murderer and cannibal, abandoning all ideas of morality to his dark and selfish desires. The rich Christopher Weldon has a reckless disregard for moral principles and the feelings of others. The affluent judge, owner of a 'fortified house', is cruel and evil, gaining sadistic pleasure from the sight of the hangman's rope in his dining room.

In contrast, love, warmth, generosity and kindness seem the preserve of the poorer people, especially the servants. Shepherd Fennel exemplifies the natural courtesy and generosity of the ordinary folk.

The penal system

The penal system which did so much to preserve the power and wealth of the rich, is severely criticised. Its three representatives are the Judge, the foolish, incompetent constable in *The Three Strangers,* and the hangman in the same story. He is insensitively proud of his distasteful job, patronising about the locals, but prepared to exploit their hospitality. We never forget that his work involves killing poor people for stealing sheep to feed their hungry families.

DUTY AND DEVOTION

On a more optimistic note, human beings are shown to be capable of love and devotion over a long period, and several are stoical in the face of misfortune. Isaac Scatchard is one such, who shows admirable fortitude and strong moral principles. He will not break a promise, and he shows love and compassion for his mother. She in return loves and protects him, which enables Isaac to survive. Several stories demonstrate the strength of maternal love, or equally strong affection from a mother-substitute such as Hester.

Hester shows the positive power of such love, and, although Samuel Lowgood is not a wholly attractive character, his devotion is impressive. Duty and obligation, described in several stories, were much-admired Victorian values.

THE INDIVIDUAL STRUGGLE

Both American stories feature a hero who is sentenced to death for trying to follow his conscience. Emphasis on individual conscience and freedom is a strong feature of American culture.

You may notice a difference of emphasis between the British stories and the American ones of Edgar Allan Poe and Ambrose Bierce. American fiction is frequently about an individual struggling for survival in a harsh environment, reflecting both the experience of many Americans in a challenging new country in the nineteenth century and the individualism of the culture, whereas British fiction focuses on social relationships.

Both American stories describe an individual trying to escape apparently certain death and emphasise how the **protagonist** (see Literary Terms) reacts to the danger, which, unlike in the British stories, is entirely natural and human. Edgar Allan Poe's narrator faces many dangers, but no ghosts!

T HE POPULARITY OF MYSTERY STORIES

Many of these stories contain a mystery or confusion which is resolved at the end of the story. It is no accident that the mystery and detective stories enjoyed particular popularity in the late nineteenth century. As mentioned in Context and Setting, this was an age of confusion and anxiety, when the certainties of the past were challenged. The conservative Victorians liked certainty and disliked confusion. It was reassuring for them to read that mysteries could be solved, with the truth being revealed at the end. One reason Sherlock Holmes was so popular was that he could solve the most intractable problems by the use of reason and intelligence.

What moral messages do you think are conveyed by the plot and conclusion of 'The Case of the Engineer's Thumb'?

Holmes also maintained the stability of society against the activities of antisocial criminals. There was little more devastating to middle-class Victorians than the thought that someone could counterfeit money which could be passed on to them, or that it was possible (literally) to make money without working for it. Sherlock Holmes would have helped them to sleep easily in their beds by showing that devious moves like this were doomed to failure.

S TRUCTURE

Short stories have no fixed length. Several of these stories are over twenty pages long, while the final two are under ten pages.

To some extent the structure of a short story is dictated by its relative brevity. The focus is usually on a short period of time, and sometimes on a single event. As *Samuel Lowgood's Revenge* shows, it is possible for the time scale to be several years, but the focus still tends to be on a limited number of incidents.

Unlike in the novel, there is usually just one plot and there are commonly no more than two or three locations, which are not described in detail. A few well-chosen and **evocative** (see Literary Terms) words have to stimulate the reader's imagination. If, as in *The Pit and the Pendulum* or *The Red Room*, most of the story takes place in one important setting, the author can provide more detail.

Setting

Note how important setting is in many of these stories. Lots of the ghost stories are set in lonely places or old houses and *The Signalman* depends on its setting for its atmosphere.

Epiphanies

You will sometimes find that a short story describes a moment of illumination, an **epiphany** (see Literary Terms) as it is sometimes called, when one of the characters comes to a new understanding about a situation, character or issue. Some of these stories highlight a moment of epiphany about the supernatural for a sceptical male.

Telling not showing

Short story writers don't have space for long **dialogues** (see Literary Terms) to reveal characters, so they tend to tell readers about them.

Plot is paramount

In mystery stories, the plot is of greatest importance. It must be taut and well-constructed, with an effective 'hook' at the beginning to capture the reader's interest, and a dramatic climax, often with a surprise **'twist in the tail'** (see Literary Terms).

Novels of sensation

Many of the stories written after 1860 were influenced by the **sensation novels** (see Literary Terms), with their dramatic and sensational events.

CHARACTERS

One of the differences between a novel and a short story is that the latter is unable to reveal characters in their full complexity. In stories there are generally fewer characters than in novels, but writers can provide only broad outlines of them.

As in novels, in stories there may be major and minor characters. For example, the signalman is a major character, because he figures prominently in the action, whereas the engine driver is a minor character.

It is probable that you will be asked to write about the characters in a text you are studying. The first thing to remember is that they are not real people in the real world, but imaginary characters in a fictional world created by the author. You have to evaluate characters in the context of the world of the text.

HOW CHARACTERS ARE REVEALED

There are five important ways in which authors reveal a character to the readers. These are:

- By the things the character says herself or himself, and the way in which they are said. This can be evaluated in passages of **monologue** and **dialogue** (see Literary Terms).
- By the author's descriptions of the character's innermost thoughts and feelings. This is particularly important in several of the stories in this collection, where a character is alone in a testing situation.
- By what the other characters say about the person. You need to be selective in the weight you place on the opinions of particular characters, and should not take all comments at face value. Remember that, in real life, our comments about someone may be influenced by our emotions. If we are bitter or jealous about a person, we may not be able to judge her or his behaviour objectively and fairly. Similarly, we cannot be sure all Samuel Lowgood's criticisms of

Christopher Weldon are fair, because Samuel is predisposed to see the worst in his rival.

- By the author's direct comments about the character. In this case, readers are told what they ought to think by the **omniscient narrator** (see Literary Terms). Authors vary in the amount of direct comment they make, but most nineteenth-century writers tell readers about their characters rather than allowing them to decide.

- By the character's actions, which are probably the most accurate indication of a person's true nature.

Most writers describe a character's appearance, and you will sometimes find that physical appearance is the outward manifestation of personality.

Writers sometimes use stock or stereotyped characters, knowing certain words will trigger a cluster of associations in readers. For instance, Sir Arthur Conan Doyle knew his readers would ascribe a set of characteristics to Stark as soon as his German accent was mentioned.

LANGUAGE AND STYLE

From our perspective, the language and style of most nineteenth century writers is formal, and the vocabulary complex. Sentences tend to be long, with a number of **subordinate clauses** (see Literary Terms) adding to the main idea of the sentence.

However there are profound differences between these writers. Thomas Hardy's sentences are elaborate, whereas those of Ambrose Bierce, a professional journalist, are as clipped and direct as those we are used to at the end of the twentieth century. Look at the opening section of *An Occurrence at Owl Creek Bridge* and you will see a series of simple direct statements, using largely concrete words, and few adjectives and adverbs.

Guy de Maupassant, too, is different from most of the writers. His story, after the initial section which sets the scene, reads like an accident report in a newspaper. It is flat, restrained, unemotional and uses simple vocabulary.

Compare the sentence structure of Poe and Hardy with that of Maupassant. What differences are there?

Thomas Hardy was a major poet, and he is frequently capable of a stunningly beautiful and **evocative** (see Literary Terms) word or image. The **simile** (see Literary Terms) 'blown inside-out like umbrellas' (p. 131) to describe the wind-swept tails of the birds, illustrates this.

Pathetic fallacy

You may have noticed the link between weather and the action. Supernatural events seem to coincide with wind and snow in a version of the **pathetic fallacy** (see Literary Terms).

PART FOUR

Study skills

How to use quotations

One of the secrets of success in writing essays is the way you use quotations. There are five basic principles:

- Put inverted commas at the beginning and end of the quotation
- Write the quotation exactly as it appears in the original
- Do not use a quotation that repeats what you have just written
- Use the quotation so that it fits into your sentence
- Keep the quotation as short as possible

Quotations should be used to develop the line of thought in your essays.

Your comment should not duplicate what is in your quotation. For example:

The description of the signalman tells us that he was dark and sallow, with a black beard and bushy eyebrows, 'he was a dark sallow man, with a dark beard and rather heavy eyebrows'.

Far more effective is to write:

When he first meets the signalman, the narrator describes him as a 'dark sallow man, with a dark beard and rather heavy eyebrows'.

However, the most sophisticated way of using the writer's words is to embed them into your sentence:

The signalman must have been a striking figure, with his 'dark beard' and 'rather heavy eyebrows'.

When you use quotations in this way, you are demonstrating the ability to use text as evidence to support your ideas - not simply including words from the original to prove you have read it.

Everyone writes differently. Work through the suggestions given here and adapt the advice to suit your own style and interests. This will improve your essay-writing skills and allow your personal voice to emerge.

The following points indicate in ascending order the skills of essay writing:

- Picking out one or two facts about the story and adding the odd detail
- Writing about the text by retelling the story
- Retelling the story and adding a quotation here and there
- Organising an answer which explains what is happening in the text and giving quotations to support what you write

....

- Writing in such a way as to show that you have thought about the intentions of the writer of the text and that you understand the techniques used
- Writing at some length, giving your viewpoint on the text and commenting by picking out details to support your views
- Looking at the text as a work of art, demonstrating clear critical judgement and explaining to the reader of your essay how the enjoyment of the text is assisted by literary devices, linguistic effects and psychological insights; showing how the text relates to the time when it was written

The dotted line above represents the division between lower and higher level grades. Higher-level performance begins when you start to consider your response as a reader of the text. The highest level is reached when you offer an enthusiastic personal response and show how this piece of literature is a product of its time.

Coursework
essay

Set aside an hour or so at the start of your work to plan what you have to do.

- List all the points you feel are needed to cover the task. Collect page references of information and quotations that will support what you have to say. A helpful tool is the highlighter pen: this saves painstaking copying and enables you to target precisely what you want to use.

- Focus on what you consider to be the main points of the essay. Try to sum up your argument in a single sentence, which could be the closing sentence of your essay. Depending on the essay title, it could be a statement about a character: The signalman is a conscientious and painstaking man who is tortured by the fear that he will be responsible for an accident if he doesn't respond to the ghostly warning; an opinion about setting: the enclosed nature of the cutting and tunnel contribute to the feeling that the signalman is trapped and isolated from human support; or a judgement on a theme: the theme of male scepticism about the power of ghosts is illustrated by Abney in *Lost Hearts* and Malcolmson in *The Judge's House*, for they both ignore the danger of supernatural revenge.

- Make a short essay plan. Use the first paragraph to introduce the argument you wish to make. In the following paragraphs develop this argument with details, examples and other possible points of view. Sum up your argument in the last paragraph. Check you have answered the question.

- Write the essay, remembering all the time the central point you are making.

- On completion, go back over what you have written to eliminate careless errors and improve expression. Read it aloud to yourself, or, if you are feeling more confident, to a relative or friend.

If you can, try to type your essay, using a word processor. This will allow you to correct and improve your writing without spoiling its appearance.

Examination essay

The essay written in an examination often carries more marks than the coursework essay even though it is written under considerable time pressure.

In the revision period build up notes on various aspects of the text you are using. Fortunately, in acquiring this set of York Notes on *Mystery Stories of the Nineteenth Century*, you have made a prudent beginning! York Notes are set out to give you vital information and help you to construct your personal overview of the text.

Make notes with appropriate quotations about the key issues of the set text. Go into the examination knowing your text and having a clear set of opinions about it.

In most English Literature examinations you can take in copies of your set books. This in an enormous advantage although it may lull you into a false sense of security. Beware! There is simply not enough time in an examination to read the book from scratch.

In the examination

- Read the question paper carefully and remind yourself what you have to do.
- Look at the questions on your set texts to select the one that most interests you and mentally work out the points you wish to stress.
- Remind yourself of the time available and how you are going to use it.
- Briefly map out a short plan in note form that will keep your writing on track and illustrate the key argument you want to make.
- Then set about writing it.
- When you have finished, check through to eliminate errors.

To summarise, • Know the text
these are the • Have a clear understanding of and opinions on the storyline,
keys to success: characters, setting, themes and writer's concerns
                   • Select the right material
                   • Plan and write a clear response, continually bearing the question
                     in mind

Sample essay plan

A typical essay question on *Mystery Stories of the Nineteenth Century* is followed by a sample essay plan in note form. This does not present the only answer to the question, merely one answer. Don't be afraid to include your own ideas, and leave out some of those in the sample! Remember that quotations are essential to prove and illustrate the points you make.

Discuss the treatment of the theme of revenge in some stories in *Mystery Stories of the Nineteenth Century*.

Introduction   Revenge has been a common theme in literature. The concept of vengeance, of 'an eye for an eye', was enshrined in ancient religion and law, giving some kind of legitimacy to the search for revenge.

Paragraph 1   Several stories cover this theme. They are: *A Vendetta, The Old Nurse's Story, Lost Hearts, Samuel Lowgood's Revenge, The Judge's House* and *The Ostler*.

Paragraph 2   Revenge is an exceptionally powerful emotion. It drives people to extreme and uncharacteristic actions, and is sometimes self-destructive. Examples are the widow Saverini, Grace Furnivall, Samuel Lowgood and possibly Rebecca Scatchard.

Paragraph 3   Revenge isn't always perpetrated on the real offender. Grace and Maude Furnivall take revenge on each other, when the real offenders are the males, their father and their lover.

Paragraph 4   The desire for revenge may be linked to excessive pride and irrational jealousy. Maude and Grace are too proud to abandon their competition, and Samuel Lowgood is initially jealous of Christopher Weldon for his beauty and elegance.

Paragraph 5   Revenge may involve reactions out of all proportion to the original offence. All Malcolmson has done is take up residence in the Judge's house, and Isaac Scatchard has done little to warrant the murderous attack on him. It may sometimes take such control of a person that vengeance continues beyond death.

Paragraph 6   A couple of stories suggest that vengeance may be justified in certain circumstances. This is when it appears to be a manifestation of natural justice as in the case of the killings of Abney in *Lost Hearts* and Ravolati in *A Vendetta*. In both cases individual action seems inevitable because justice has not been achieved through the legal system. *The Three Strangers* implies the legal system is constructed to wreak vengeance on the poor.

Conclusion   These stories testify to the power of revenge, an emotion that exists beyond the reach of the rational mind. Although we are told God said 'Vengeance is mine', some people cannot wait.

FURTHER QUESTIONS

Make a plan as shown above and attempt these questions.

1 Discuss the relationship between Samuel Lowgood and Christopher Weldon, and illustrate how, and for what reasons, it changes during the course of the story.

2 By looking in detail at *The Signalman* and at least one other story, show how authors can create

atmosphere and a vivid setting by their choice of words and images.

3 Imagine that Barbox Brothers, the narrator of *The Signalman*, has either been asked to present written evidence of the events leading to the signalman's death for the official accident inquiry, or wants to include the incident in his autobiography. Please write one of these for him.

4 In her circumstances, and given the values of nineteenth-century Britain, do you feel any sympathy for Rebecca Scatchard?

5 Compare the attitudes to the supernatural shown in at least three of the short stories.

6 Choose two stories with a first person narrator and evaluate the effect of this technique on your response to the plot, characters and themes.

7 What impression of Victorian life and vlaues have you gained from these stories?

8 Please write an account of the first meeting of the signalman and Barbox Brothers, using the signalman as the narrator.

9 Choose two stories you found frightening, and describe how the author creates fear in the readers.

10 Compare two characters you think are very different in background, personality and beliefs.

PART FIVE

CULTURAL CONNECTIONS

BROADER PERSPECTIVES

James felt that fictional ghosts are more frightening when 'seen' in daylight. The usual background in nineteenth-century ghost stories was night and often moonlight.

Library bookshelves groan with collections of ghost, mystery and detective stories of the nineteenth and twentieth century. The most famous classic ghost stories not in this collection are probably *The Turn of the Screw* by Henry James (Penguin, 1994 – first published 1898), and *The Monkey's Paw* by W.W. Jacobs (Robin Clarke, 1994 – first published 1902). The former was influenced by *The Old Nurse's Story*. Do not read either if, like me, you are of a nervous disposition!

Detective stories have been very popular in recent times. The list is endless, but a good place to begin would be with Colin Dexter's novels featuring Inspector Morse, also a great television favourite.

Roald Dahl was a clever and imaginative recent writer of mystery stories, and I especially like his *Lamb to the Slaughter* (Michael Joseph, 1954) and *The Hitchhiker* (Jonathan Cape, 1977).

Several of Dahl's stories were dramatised in *Tales of the Unexpected* on television, and Wilkie Collins's *The Woman in White* (Penguin, 1994 – first published 1860) and *The Moonstone* (Penguin, 1994 – first published 1868) have been broadcast. Videotapes of these, and of the dramatisation of *The Signalman*, should be available. There have been film versions of *The Pit and the Pendulum* (e.g. the 1961 version starring Vincent Price and John Kerr) and of other Edgar Allan Poe stories. *The Turn of the Screw* was filmed as *The Innocents* (e.g. the 1961 version starring Deborah Kerr and Peter Wingarde).

If you want to pursue an interest in a particular author,

you will find it easiest to obtain the selected ghost stories of Charles Dickens (Pocket Classics) and M.R. James (Wordsworth Classics). Six of Ambrose Bierce's stories are in the Penguin 60s series. There are paperback editions of Thomas Hardy's *Wessex Tales* (Wordsworth, 1995 – first published 1888), and Sir Arthur Conan Doyle's Sherlock Holmes stories and Edgar Allan Poe's *Tales of Mystery and Imagination* are readily available (e.g. Wordsworth 1992).

You may want to read the following novels which will give you an insight into Victorian fiction and/or the horror genre:

Frankenstein by Mary Shelley (Penguin, 1994 – first published 1818)

Dracula by Bram Stoker (Penguin, 1994 – first published 1897)

Wuthering Heights by Emily Brontë (Penguin, 1965 – first published 1847)

Mary Barton by Elizabeth Gaskell (Penguin, 1968 – first published 1848)

Jane Eyre by Charlotte Brontë (Penguin, 1966 – first published 1847)

Tess of the d'Urbervilles by Thomas Hardy (Penguin, 1994 – first published 1891)

Audio tapes   A couple of the stories are available on audio tapes:

The Old Nurse's Story is available on *English Short Stories 1800–1900* (Penguin, Audiobooks)

The Signalman is available on *Classic Tales of the Paranormal* (CSA Telltapes)

World events		Authors and stories
Industrial Revolution begins in Britain. For the next 100 years people will move from the countryside to industrialised towns	1750	
Napoleon becomes Emperor of France	1804	
	1809	Birth of Edgar Allan Poe
	1810	Birth of Elizabeth Gaskell
	1812	Birth of Charles Dickens
Battle of Waterloo	1815	
Napoleon dies in captivity on St Helena	1823	
	1824	Birth of Wilkie Collins
In Russia an unsuccessful revolt against the Tsar. First railway trains	1825	
	1831	Birth of Amelia Edwards
First Reform Bill	1832	
Britain abolishes slavery	1833	
	1835	Birth of Mary E. Braddon
Victoria becomes Queen Invention of photography	1837	
	1840	Birth of Thomas Hardy
	1842	Birth of Ambrose Bierce
	1843	*The Pit and the Pendulum*
	1847	Birth of Bram Stoker
Karl Marx: *Manifesto of Communism* Right of women to vote first proposed in United States	1848	
	1850	Birth of Guy de Maupassant
	1852	*The Old Nurse's Story* *The Phantom Coach*
Crimean War	1853-6	
	1855	*The Ostler*
Charles Darwin publishes *On the Origin of Species*	1859	Birth of Arthur Conan Doyle

World events		Authors and stories
Emancipation of Serfs in Russia	**1861**	
American Civil War	**1861-5**	
	1862	Birth of M.R. James
		Samuel Lowgood's Revenge
Abraham Lincoln, the American president, assassinated. First bicycle	**1865**	
	1866	Birth of H.G. Wells; *The Signalman*
John Stuart Mill argues for women's right to vote in Britain	**1869**	
Revolutionary Commune in Paris demands economic reforms	**1871**	
First typewriters	**1873**	
First telephone in use	**1877**	
Assassination of Tsar Alexander II in Russia	**1881**	
	1883	*The Three Strangers*
Fabian Society founded in England to promote evolutionary socialism	**1884**	
First petrol-driven car	**1885**	*A Vendetta*
	1891	*An Occurence at Owl Creek Bridge; The Judge's House*
	1892	*The Adventure of the Engineer's Thumb*
The first silent films shown	**1895**	*Lost Hearts*
	1896	*The Red Room*
Death of Queen Victoria	**1901**	
Movement for women's right to vote founded by Mrs Pankhurst	**1903**	
First Russian Revolution	**1905**	
First World War	**1914-18**	
The 'October Revolution' in Russia	**1917**	
Women over 30 granted right to vote in Britain	**1918**	
First regular radio broadcasts	**1922**	

archaic words of an earlier period which are no longer in general use when the story is written

dénouement the final unfolding of the plot, during which mysteries are solved and secrets revealed

dialogue conversation between two or more characters

epiphany moment of sudden insight, understanding or revelation

evocative words, smells, music etc. which inspire powerful memories, responses or images

feminist critique systematic examination of a text for what it reveals about gender issues and women's situation

first person narrator the story is told in the first person, using 'I', by one of the characters

Gothic novels novels, usually set in medieval times, with violent, bizarre, and often supernatural incidents. Several were written between 1750 and 1830

imagery the use of metaphors, similes and other devices to make writing more vivid and effective

irony/ironic irony is saying one thing when you mean another. In an ironic comment there are at least two layers of meaning – the surface meaning and the one below the surface

litotes achieving an effect by the use of understatement. An affirmative is expressed by using its opposite preceded by a negative. An example is using 'not good' when something is 'bad'

melodramatic sensational and improbable events in a plot

metaphor(ical) a comparison between two things without using comparing words such as 'like' or 'as'

monologue one person speaking, either with or without listeners

omniscient narrator narrating a story in the third person with total knowledge of all the characters and events

onomatopoeia words which sound like the noise they describe

pathetic fallacy the mood of Nature reflects and parallels the mood of a character in the story

protagonist the main character in a story, novel or play

pun a word which has two or more meanings

rhetorical question a question which requires no answer

satire ridiculing the behaviour and attitudes of individuals and societies

sensation novels popular novels of the 1860s which had sensational plots and incidents

simile a comparison of one thing with another, using 'like' or 'as'

subordinate clause group of words within a sentence which is subsidiary to the main idea of the sentence

symbol(ic) an object used to represent an abstract thing, such as an idea or a belief

telling or showing an author can tell the reader what to think about a character or situation, or show, without comment, a character behaving or speaking in a particular way

themes the central ideas and topics which the writer wishes to raise in the story

tragedy a story which describes the downfall of a basically good person, with the strong sense that his or her fate is predestined

'twist in the tail' unexpected developments in the plot at the end of a story

TEST ANSWERS

TEST YOURSELF (Section I)

A 1 Rebecca Murdoch *(The Ostler)*
••• 2 Grace Furnivall *(The Old Nurse's Story)*
3 Sherlock Holmes *(The Adventure of the Engineer's Thumb)*
4 Isaac Scatchard *(The Ostler)*
5 The phantom child *(The Old Nurse's Story)*
6 Elise *(The Adventure of the Engineer's Thumb)*

TEST YOURSELF (Section II)

A 1 The narrator *(The Pit and the Pendulum)*
••• 2 Lucy Malden *(Samuel Lowgood's Revenge)*
3 The engine driver *(The Signalman)*
4 The rats *(The Pit and the Pendulum)*
5 Christopher Weldon *(Samuel Lowgood's Revenge)*
6 The signalman *(The Signalman)*

TEST YOURSELF (Section III)

A 1 Mrs Bunch *(Lost Hearts)*
••• 2 The hedge-carpenter *(The Three Strangers)*
3 Dr Thornhill *(The Judge's House)*
4 The Federal scout *(An Occurrence at Owl Creek Bridge)*
5 Mr Abney *(Lost Hearts)*
6 The first stranger (the escaped prisoner) *(The Three Strangers)*
7 The judge *(The Judge's House)*
8 Peyton Farquhar *(An Occurrence at Owl Creek Bridge)*

TEST YOURSELF (Section IV)

A 1 Jacob *(The Phantom Coach)*
••• 2 The widow Saverini *(A Vendetta)*
3 The old woman *(The Red Room)*
4 A passenger *(The Phantom Coach)*
5 Antoine Saverini *(A Vendetta)*
6 The second old man *(The Red Room)*

NOTES

GCSE and equivalent levels (£3.50 each)

Maya Angelou
I Know Why the Caged Bird Sings

Jane Austen
Pride and Prejudice

Alan Ayckbourn
Absent Friends

Elizabeth Barrett Browning
Selected Poems

Robert Bolt
A Man for All Seasons

Harold Brighouse
Hobson's Choice

Charlotte Brontë
Jane Eyre

Emily Brontë
Wuthering Heights

Shelagh Delaney
A Taste of Honey

Charles Dickens
David Copperfield

Charles Dickens
Great Expectations

Charles Dickens
Hard Times

Charles Dickens
Oliver Twist

Roddy Doyle
Paddy Clarke Ha Ha Ha

George Eliot
Silas Marner

George Eliot
The Mill on the Floss

William Golding
Lord of the Flies

Oliver Goldsmith
She Stoops To Conquer

Willis Hall
The Long and the Short and the Tall

Thomas Hardy
Far from the Madding Crowd

Thomas Hardy
The Mayor of Casterbridge

Thomas Hardy
Tess of the d'Urbervilles

Thomas Hardy
The Withered Arm and other Wessex Tales

L.P. Hartley
The Go-Between

Seamus Heaney
Selected Poems

Susan Hill
I'm the King of the Castle

Barry Hines
A Kestrel for a Knave

Louise Lawrence
Children of the Dust

Harper Lee
To Kill a Mockingbird

Laurie Lee
Cider with Rosie

Arthur Miller
The Crucible

Arthur Miller
A View from the Bridge

Robert O'Brien
Z for Zachariah

Frank O'Connor
My Oedipus Complex and other stories

George Orwell
Animal Farm

J.B. Priestley
An Inspector Calls

Willy Russell
Educating Rita

Willy Russell
Our Day Out

J.D. Salinger
The Catcher in the Rye

William Shakespeare
Henry IV Part 1

William Shakespeare
Henry V

William Shakespeare
Julius Caesar

William Shakespeare
Macbeth

William Shakespeare
The Merchant of Venice

William Shakespeare
A Midsummer Night's Dream

William Shakespeare
Much Ado About Nothing

William Shakespeare
Romeo and Juliet

William Shakespeare
The Tempest

William Shakespeare
Twelfth Night

George Bernard Shaw
Pygmalion

Mary Shelley
Frankenstein

R.C. Sherriff
Journey's End

Rukshana Smith
Salt on the snow

John Steinbeck
Of Mice and Men

Robert Louis Stevenson
Dr Jekyll and Mr Hyde

Jonathan Swift
Gulliver's Travels

Robert Swindells
Daz 4 Zoe

Mildred D. Taylor
Roll of Thunder, Hear My Cry

Mark Twain
Huckleberry Finn

James Watson
Talking in Whispers

William Wordsworth
Selected Poems

A Choice of Poets

Mystery Stories of the Nineteenth Century including The Signalman

Nineteenth Century Short Stories

Poetry of the First World War

Six Women Poets

York Notes Advanced (£3.99 each)

Margaret Atwood
The Handmaid's Tale

Jane Austen
Mansfield Park

Jane Austen
Persuasion

Jane Austen
Pride and Prejudice

Alan Bennett
Talking Heads

William Blake
*Songs of Innocence and of
Experience*

Charlotte Brontë
Jane Eyre

Emily Brontë
Wuthering Heights

Geoffrey Chaucer
The Franklin's Tale

Geoffrey Chaucer
*General Prologue to the
Canterbury Tales*

Geoffrey Chaucer
*The Wife of Bath's Prologue
and Tale*

Joseph Conrad
Heart of Darkness

Charles Dickens
Great Expectations

John Donne
Selected Poems

George Eliot
The Mill on the Floss

F. Scott Fitzgerald
The Great Gatsby

E.M. Forster
A Passage to India

Brian Friel
Translations

Thomas Hardy
The Mayor of Casterbridge

Thomas Hardy
Tess of the d'Urbervilles

Seamus Heaney
*Selected Poems from Opened
Ground*

Nathaniel Hawthorne
The Scarlet Letter

James Joyce
Dubliners

John Keats
Selected Poems

Christopher Marlowe
Doctor Faustus

Arthur Miller
Death of a Salesman

Toni Morrison
Beloved

William Shakespeare
Antony and Cleopatra

William Shakespeare
As You Like It

William Shakespeare
Hamlet

William Shakespeare
King Lear

William Shakespeare
Measure for Measure

William Shakespeare
The Merchant of Venice

William Shakespeare
Much Ado About Nothing

William Shakespeare
Othello

William Shakespeare
Romeo and Juliet

William Shakespeare
The Tempest

William Shakespeare
The Winter's Tale

Mary Shelley
Frankenstein

Alice Walker
The Color Purple

Oscar Wilde
*The Importance of Being
Earnest*

Tennessee Williams
A Streetcar Named Desire

John Webster
The Duchess of Malfi

W.B. Yeats
Selected Poems

RIVER OF NO REPRIEVE

Books by Jeffrey Tayler

Siberian Dawn

Facing the Congo

Glory in a Camel's Eye

Angry Wind

River of No Reprieve